When I Whisper, Nobody Listens

When I Whisper, Nobody Listens

Helping Young People Write About Difficult Issues

HELEN FROST

HEINEMANN
Portsmouth, NH

Heinemann
A division of Reed Elsevier Inc.
361 Hanover Street
Portsmouth, NH 03081–3912
www.heinemann.com

Offices and agents throughout the world

The author and publisher wish to thank those who have generously given permission to reprint borrowed material:

"Rule One" from *Lifelines* by Philip Booth. Copyright © 1999 by Philip Booth. Used by permission of Viking Penguin, a division of Penguin Putnam, Inc.

"The Portrait" from *Passing Through: The Later Poems New and Selected* by Stanley Kunitz. Copyright © 1971 by Stanley Kunitz. Used by permission of W. W. Norton & Company, Inc.

"Middle Sister Poem" by Ingrid Wendt. Copyright © 1987 by Ingrid Wendt. First appeared in *Singing the Mozart Requiem* published by Breitenbush Books, Inc. Used by permission of the author.

"Kerosene" from *Hammerlock* by Timothy Seibles. Copyright by Timothy Seibles. Published by the Cleveland State University Poetry Center. Used by permission of the author.

"Watermelon Hill" by Linda Back McKay. Copyright Linda Back McKay. Used by permission of the author.

"I Remember Mrs. King" by Ketu Oladuwa. Copyright by Ketu Oladuwa. Used by permission of the author.

"The Universe is a Safe Place for Souls" from *Flatlands* by Jeff Gundy. Copyright by Jeff Gundy. Published by the Cleveland State University Poetry Center. Used by permission of the author.

"Sap" by Beth Lee Simon. Copyright by Beth Lee Simon. First published in *TriQuarterly* 90, 1994. Used by permission of the author.

"River of Choices" by Maralee Martin. Copyright by the Center for Nonviolence, Fort Wayne, Indiana. Used by permission of Maralee Martin.

Excerpt from the manuscript *Oh My Darlin* by Claire Ewart. Copyright by Claire Ewart. Used by permission of the author.

"Eat Dirt" by Constance García-Barrio. Copyright by Constance García-Barrio. First published in the *Kerf Literary Review*, June 1998. Used by permission of the author.

Scenes 5 and 7 from *Why Darkness Seems So Light* by Helen Frost and Harvey Cocks. Copyright © 1999 by Pioneer Drama Service, Inc. Used by permission of Pioneer Drama Service, Inc. For information on performance rights or how to purchase copies of the play, contact Pioneer Drama Service, Inc., P.O. Box 4267, Englewood, CO 80155-4267.

Library of Congress Cataloging-in-Publication Data
Frost, Helen.
When I whisper nobody listens : helping young people write about difficult issues / Helen Frost.
p. cm.
ISBN 0-325-00352-1 (alk. paper)
1. English language — Rhetoric — Study and teaching — Psychological aspects.
2. English language — Composition and exercises — Study and teaching — Psychological aspects. 3. Creative writing — Study and teaching — Psychological aspects. 4. Youth — Conduct of life. 5. Youth — Psychology. 6. Youth and violence. I. Title.
PE1404 .F75 2001
808'.042'071 — dc21   2001024854

Editor: Danny Miller
Production editor: Sonja S. Chapman
Cover design: Joni Doherty, Joni Doherty Design
Manufacturing: Steve Bernier

Printed in the United States of America on acid-free paper
05 04 03 02 01   RRD   1 2 3 4 5

Dedicated to four remarkable teachers

Pebble Brooks
Susan Harroff
Ingrid Wendt
Kathyrn Willcutt

No one ever knows
How much another hurts.
                    . . .
Or maybe in a thousand, one
Has the toughness to,
                            to care,
to give beyond a selfish pity.
        —Philip Booth, from "Rule One"

Contents

Five

Six

PART THREE:
WRITING ACTIVITIES

Seven

Eight

Nine

Ten

Appendix A

Appendix B

Appendix C

Appendix D

Acknowledgments

My gratitude goes back and back. I remember the adults who listened to me when I was a child: Uncle Gay, Aunt Esther, my parents and older sisters, a few early teachers. On through high school and Syracuse University, where Bob Davis encouraged me to teach and Philip Booth encouraged me to write and Gretchen McManus encouraged me to find ways of putting the two together.

Throughout my adult life, teaching and writing have been woven together, and my greatest passion has always been in the intersections: teaching writing, writing about teaching, and now here I have been given this chance to write about teaching writing! Countless people supported me as the book came to fruition.

Thank you, Harvey Cocks, Becky Hill, Kris Richey, Palmer Hall, and all the administrators, the teachers, and the students who worked with me on *Why Darkness Seems So Light: Young People Speak Out About Violence*. And thank you, Virginia Juettner, for seeing the value of that project, suggesting that I write a book about it, and putting me in touch with Heinemann editors.

My artist colleagues, John Beams, Ketu Oladuwa, and Lisa Tsetse, have supported me for many years in our work with at-risk youth; if you hear a drumbeat behind the student writing, or if you sense that the creative mind is opened by the body's work, or if you see a handful of clay within the shape of a poem or a story, this is because my work with young people is, at its best, one part of an artistic whole, crafted with these dear friends. Many of the writing exercises I describe were developed in our work together, and I can't say what were my own ideas and what came from others. The support of that work through CAP-V grants from Arts United of Greater Fort Wayne, funded by the Lincoln National Foundation and the Foellinger Foundation, has been essential; recently the work has also been supported by several grants from the National Endowment for the Arts and others.

The staff at the Center for Nonviolence in Fort Wayne, Indiana, has developed a strong curriculum that often uses writing to address issues of violence, and I thank them for what I have learned from them, as well as for allowing me to quote them and adapt their River of Choices activity.

Several people read and consulted with me about Chapter 3, "Legal and Ethical Concerns." I thank Karla K. Koomler, guidance counselor at Butler Eastside Junior-Senior High School, for support through the years, as well as for reading Chapter 3. I also met with administrators of Fort Wayne Community Schools: Greg Slyford, Manager of Guidance and Testing, and Marg Roberts, Specialist for Case Managers. I am grateful for help and advice from all these people, but I wish to clarify that nothing they said, and nothing I have written, should be interpreted as legal advice. If you have legal or ethical questions regarding your own work, please seek appropriate counsel in your own community.

Elizabeth Smith-Meyer read Chapter 10 and offered suggestions about teaching fiction writing, and I thank her.

Over many years, I have worked with countless writers and teachers throughout the country, and I have read hundreds of books and articles about teaching writing. It is impossible to trace the origins of poetic forms or teaching ideas, and even those ideas that I believe to be original have undoubtedly occurred to others. I am grateful for this lifelong collaboration, and I especially appreciate Ingrid Wendt, whose book *Starting with Little Things* has been a steady source of inspiration.

Many excellent writers have allowed me to use their work as examples in this book and I am grateful for their generosity. The adult authors whose work appears in the example sections have written notes regarding their work, and given permission for teachers to photocopy the work and the notes for classroom use. Please include a publication credit with any work you photocopy. In some cases, pseudonyms are used with student work.

I thank teacher-photographer Susan Harroff and the students and parents who gave permission to include photographs. I wish to make it clear that most of the students in the photographs are not the same students whose writing appears in the book; please do not assume that the young people in the photographs are writing about traumatic or difficult experiences.

Danny Miller, Heinemann editor, has seen this book through from beginning to end, helping shape the proposal and working with me, section by section and chapter by chapter, to refine the details. His hard work, careful reading, clear suggestions, and infinite patience are the backbone of the book, and I thank him.

My husband, Chad Thompson, and our children, Lloyd and Glen, support me in countless ways, in my work with young writers and in my own writing. And my parents, Jack and Jean Frost, and siblings, Mary, Margaret, Kathy, Barbie, Dorothy, Nancy, Dick, Karen, and Herb, are behind my work, always, in a way that the title of this book helps me define. All my life, I have felt that, even in the midst of a busy household and a full life, someone has been available to listen to my most tentative whispers. Now we are scattered throughout the country, but our phone calls and e-mail conversations continue to be my safest sounding board.

As this book passes into your hands, may you feel the presence of other listeners, and may you feel supported in your own whispering, or in your most boisterous shout-it-out writing, as well as in your listening. I thank you for your thoughtful reading and wish you well in your compassionate teaching.

Introduction

As this book has emerged from idea, to proposal, to rough draft, to this final version, I have considered a number of titles. Something about truth, I thought, something about the difficulty of speaking the truth, especially when you are young and in a school system that doesn't always want to acknowledge your truth if it is uncomfortable or difficult to hear. I was thinking of something strident, about giving voice to young writers; I liked other books' titles with words like *shout* or *holler* in them. But that tone didn't seem quite right for this book, and I remained open to other possibilities. Then one day, a quiet young writer, handed me her poem:

> yellow rain blue paint   all mixed
> up in a splash   when I sleep
> I hear music   when I am awake
> I see dark and millions of
> spiders and a big green eye
> looking at me   when I dance
> I am a fool   when I whisper
> nobody listens
>
> *—A.H.*

The whole poem stayed with me, and the last line kept repeating itself, telling me something new: We, as teachers of writing, don't have to help our students shout out their truths; we can help them write with precision and grace, and such writing will amplify their whispers or subdue their screams, allowing them to tell whatever kind of truth they need to tell. We can support young writers as they struggle to find their most authentic voices, and we can learn to tilt our ears toward those voices and listen.

I have taught writing for more than twenty-five years, as a classroom teacher and as a visiting writer. I have received stories and poems and scripts from children and young adults in preschools, elementary schools, middle schools, high schools, universities, adolescent group homes, juvenile detention centers, and court-ordered violence-prevention programs

I love the language young writers use and the pride they take in seeing their stories on the page. I love their quirky misspellings ("pain-staking" or "pantyhoes" or "rille rille sad") and their leaps of imagination as they stretch to write whatever truths they need to tell. I love the way the writing comes alive when read aloud in a classroom — the way it settles peacefully in the room or charges the air with amazement, in delight or in compassion.

Most of the writing I receive from students is not about trauma. It is about horses, grandparents, sports, rivers, cars, love, deer hunting, little brothers, escaped gerbils. But in every classroom, no matter what the writing activity, one or two students present a piece of writing that requires special attention: a fourth grader writes about her mother crying all the time; a seventh grader uses imagery that suggests sexual abuse; a ninth grader contemplates carrying a gun; a tenth grader considers whether or not to have an abortion.

When I first received such writing, I considered it to be the exception to what I thought was the norm. I don't know whether the times have changed or my own sensitivity has sharpened, but I now believe that far more children than we would like to believe have suffered some kind of serious trauma. I would estimate that at least a third of the children in our classrooms carry burdens that will have lifelong consequences.

I base this estimate partly on a project that I undertook in the spring of 1998. I was asked by the YWCA in a medium-sized American city to work with high school students, helping them write about their experiences of violence for the purpose of writing a play to be performed as part of the YWCA's annual Week Without Violence campaign. I worked with 249 students in six high schools — urban, rural, and suburban — asking them to write about any incident in which they had been personally affected by violence. Only a handful of students told me they had nothing to write about; approximately one-third of them wrote about witnessing a murder, being raped or abused, the suicide of someone in their family, or an assault that left someone with permanent injuries.

Because the stories were so compelling, I edited an anthology, *Why Darkness Seems So Light*, to share the stories with others. The stories were also the basis of the play I co-authored with Harvey Cocks, which was presented by the local Youtheatre the following fall and published by Pioneer Drama Services about a year later.

These stories seemed to generate others. Students started to think of me as someone who would listen to—or read—those things that they could not tell anyone else. I became relatively unshockable as I learned how to offer, without prying, the opportunity to write about personal topics. I found ways to support students as they found their way into and through such writing.

At the same time, and continuing through the ensuing years to the present, I worked as part of an interdisciplinary artistic team in a violence-prevention program designed to bring together arts organizations and social service agencies. The young people selected for participation in that program are considered to be at risk for involvement in violence, so it's possible that my perception of the level of violence and other trauma among our youth is skewed by the selection process. But most of the young people in our program are also attending school. The stories they write and tell in the safe places my colleagues and I provide for them are the stories they carry with them during their school days. They work hard to keep the stories from surfacing. As a result, although most veteran teachers do have a sense that the level of trauma in their students' lives is disturbingly high, they often have no specific knowledge of what their students have been through or are going through.

Consider what we know about the level of violence in the United States and how it disproportionately affects young people. Recent statistics show that violent crime is decreasing in the United States but that youth ages twelve–nineteen are still disproportionately victimized by it. According to the 1999 federal crime report, seventy-seven out of one thousand sixteen- to nineteen-year-olds were victims of violent crime. If each of those young people has three or four siblings and cousins, plus eight or nine close friends, that means that about twenty percent of our youth have a close relationship with someone who has been a victim of murder, rape, robbery, or assault. Add the perpetrators, along with their circles of family and friends, and the numbers add up all too quickly.

There is general agreement that this level of violence is unacceptable and that lowering it should be a national priority. But what constitutes violence? How should we respond to it? On such questions, there is little agreement. Is spanking a three-year-old an act of violence or "good old-fashioned discipline"? Should we create stricter gun control laws or should we arm principals and teachers? Should we encourage unquestioning patriotism or teach students to debate the wisdom of historical decisions and policies? Should we try to control violent video games, music, television, and movies? If so, how?

Looking beyond violence to other kinds of hurt: Should you forgive someone who has hurt you? Usually? Always? Never? Does the answer depend upon the degree of hurt? Does it change if the hurt is irrevocable? If the answer is yes, how do you do it? If no, what can you do with your anger? And what if you are the one in need of forgiveness? How can you ask for it? Can you accept it?

What about the tragedies for which there can be no blame? Young people grieve the loss of friends, relatives, and pets, whatever the cause of death. And other issues trouble many of them: problems related to sexuality, drug use, responsibility for younger siblings, parental instability.

These issues are complex and interrelated. If we allow them into our classrooms, we can support our students as they struggle to face them. And what better way to open our classrooms to these issues than through written language? Writing demands focus, concentration, imagination, patience — skills that are also useful in dealing with difficult life situations.

The question then arises: Is it wise to approach personal subjects in a direct way, specifically inviting students to write about them? My response to this is not an absolute and emphatic yes, but it *is* a cautious yes. Strong taboos surround many of the things students may want to write about, and, as in the case of most taboos, good reasons exist for maintaining them. But equally substantial reasons exist for breaking them, if we can do so, and allow our students to do so, with careful respect.

When children lock away something significant in their lives and treat it as off-limits for school or conversation, they put a lot of energy into creating that separation between school/external life and off-limits/internal life. Teachers also put considerable energy into maintaining that separation, often without being aware that they are doing so.

Even one experience of allowing the internal life to be acknowledged as part of the external life can have great benefits, connecting children to their schoolwork and releasing energy they need for all their subjects. The energy of the teacher is aligned with the energy of the students, rather than in opposition to it.

When students listen respectfully to the honest story, poem, or essay of a classmate, a heart-to-heart connection is made. This encourages a combination of self-respect and respect for others that can be, in some measure, an antidote to many of the situations the students describe in their writing.

Let me offer an example of a student who asked for my help as she struggled to write about something that was difficult for her. This happened at a summer program for teenagers who had been removed from their homes, but Camille could be a student in any classroom.

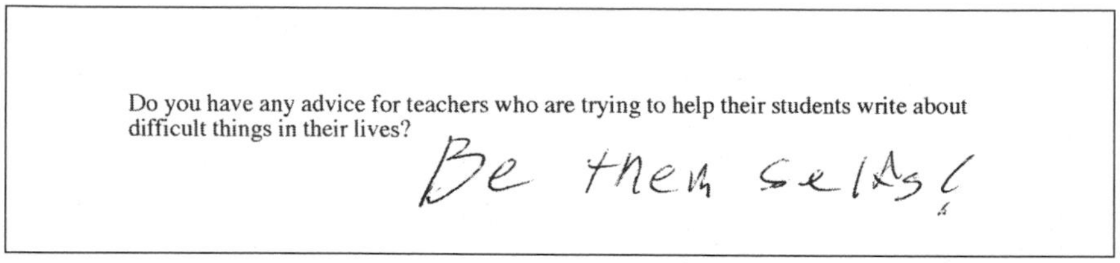

Do you have any advice for teachers who are trying to help their students write about difficult things in their lives? *Be them selfs!*

Figure I–1   It sounds easy, but it's hard advice to follow.

I was sitting on the floor of a hot gym with a group of twelve girls between the ages of eleven and seventeen. The fans above us cooled the air a little but were so noisy it was hard for us to hear one another. None of the girls in the circle that afternoon really wanted to be there; they didn't know who I was and I had only the vaguest notion of who they were—kids who, for one reason or another, couldn't live at home with their families. We started with introductions.

"I'm Helen Frost," I began. "I'm a writer, and I'm here as part of a program that brings artists together with young people who may be at risk for involvement in violence."

There. Something true had been spoken, carefully, directly, and unemotionally. It told them one tiny thing about who I am and one tiny thing I knew about them.

Half an hour later, I asked them to write a poem about something they remembered. I didn't know these girls very well yet, so I kept the task as neutral as possible. "Think of it as an invitation or a gift, not an assignment," I suggested.

Still, Camille was agitated, and as the other girls took their papers and pencils to various corners of the gym and started writing, she approached me:

"I can't write about this."

"But you can write about anything," I said, repeating the instructions. "Happy or sad, little or big. Something you remember from a long time ago or something that happened this morning."

"No, you don't understand. Something really terrible happened to me, and I can't write about it." There was a pause as I considered how to respond. "It was really, really bad," she asserted one more time.

"Well, you could write about something else."

"I can't remember anything else."

I paused again, assessing the situation. Clearly she had something she wanted desperately to tell or write or shape in some way. She couldn't confront it directly but wanted to know if there was any safe way to approach it.

She was asking me for help. I needed a little more information, but I didn't want to be intrusive. I spoke carefully.

"How old were you when this happened?"

"Fourteen."

Something very recent had changed her life; it still felt raw and tender and it was blocking out all her other memories. If Camille were a student in your classroom, she might not be able to hear a word you say, she might not be able to read or write, and she almost certainly could not tell you why.

I could see many things Camille needed at that moment, and I was aware of what I could and could not offer. I couldn't give her a safe home; I couldn't be her therapist. But I could express compassion in a pragmatic way; I could offer her a way to write about whatever was so much on her mind.

I told her, "There is a way to write about something without saying what you're writing about: Put a title on your paper, something like 'When I Was Thirteen' or 'Before I Was Fourteen,' and then write down everything you can think of about how your life was different before this event happened. In a way, you are writing about what has been taken from you, but you don't have to say how it happened. No one needs to know what you're writing about." I was guessing, but the look on her face confirmed that I was not far off.

She smiled; it must have seemed like an ingenious solution to her. She took her paper and stayed close to me as I helped other kids. Every so often she looked up, face flushed, and asked, "No one is going to read this, right?"

"Not unless you want someone to."

When we came together to share the afternoon's writing, Camille clutched her paper, folded into a fist-size square, exclaimed "No!" when I invited her to read it, and stuffed it deep into her pocket when it was time to leave. But I noticed that she was able to hear and respond to the other kids' writing. And she was glowing. Somehow, she had made this story her own. She had gained some measure of control.

For classroom teachers, such a scenario might be complicated by the need for assessment, accountability, and grades. But the benefits of helping your students write about what is important to them should be given considerable weight in the decisions you make about how to spend your classroom hours.

The benefits for students are:

- personal investment in their writing
- an element of control over some of the difficult — and often private — issues they may be facing
- a sense of connection to you and one another, all of which helps create a sense of community

Those are also benefits to you, as a teacher of writing and as a member of a classroom community. You will cut through some of the defensive posturing among your students and see what is really going on in your classroom. In so doing, you will enrich your classroom community and help foster a spirit of cooperation.

Each of you will have different concerns arising from different teaching situations. You may be confronted with issues of violence or trauma in student writing without doing anything to encourage such topics. Maybe you have assigned what seems to be a fairly safe topic, such as "Write about a childhood memory," or even the old favorite, "How I spent my summer vacation," and you find yourself reading about a child being locked in a shed for three days, or something that makes you wonder, "Just how did this dog die?" It is helpful to have given some thought to what you should do if something like that comes up. Or you may become aware of some troubling undercurrent in your classroom, and you wonder if there is a way to bring it safely, intentionally, to the surface through carefully designed writing activities. In either case, you may have questions and concerns. Among the concerns I've heard voiced and have considered while writing this book are the following:

- I teach fifth grade in a suburban elementary school. I fear that today's bully or victim of bullying will be in tomorrow's headlines about teenage gun violence. I have my students do a lot of writing, and I wonder if writing can help them learn to solve conflicts.
- I'm never sure about the best response to writing that reflects suicidal thoughts or extreme anger.
- I teach Basic English to 120 high school sophomores in an inner-city school. Their lives are drenched in guns, drugs, and violence, and my district requires me to teach them to identify metaphor, alliteration, and onomatopoeia in poems by Edgar Allen Poe and Robert Service. How can I bring my curriculum more in line with their needs?
- Students these days are so disrespectful and arrogant, I have a hard time controlling my anger toward them. I often make them write about what they did and what they could have done differently. It's a better punishment than detention because they have to practice their writing skills, and maybe it makes them think a little bit.
- I teach sixth grade in a middle school in a small rural community. I have some students who have been sheltered and protected and others who have more life experience than I do. I want to let all of them write from

their own experiences, but I don't want to be responsible for anyone's loss of innocence.

- I've worked for seventeen years in a juvenile detention facility. I listen to the stories "my kids" have to tell, and I say, "You should write that down." But I don't know how to help them do it.

- I teach ninth-grade history in a Native American community. I wonder if I could use writing to help my students understand the violence in our history and how it relates to their personal experience.

- I'm a writer and I've been asked to go into a high school after a school shooting to help the students write about the experience. Is there really any value in this, or is it just making them go through it all again? Maybe we all need to put it behind us and move on.

- I teach special ed in a small-town middle school. At this age, a lot of my students go through something I call "wheelchair rage," sudden explosions of anger at seemingly trivial frustrations. I'd like to find a way of helping them express their feelings in a safe way.

- I'm a teacher, not a social worker. If kids write about things like abuse or gang activity, am I required to report it? I'm not sure I want to take on that responsibility.

I know that writing can be useful in all of these situations, and I know that each situation requires different kinds of sensitivity, knowledge, and skill. In the following chapters, I discuss many of the questions that arise when students write about private and difficult issues, and I give philosophical and pragmatic advice that should be of use in a variety of situations.

I have tremendous respect for the challenges teachers face. As you read this book, you may find yourself thinking "Ha, that would never work with *my* students," and you might be right about specific suggestions. But in general, try to step back and see if there is anything you could do so that these ideas might work for you. I have taught writing in classrooms where teachers were extremely frustrated and students were totally disengaged—absent half the time and asleep when they were "present"; the writing activities, used with respect, have been effective even in those extreme situations.

If we can teach our students to use language truthfully, skillfully, and perhaps beautifully, we offer them a power quite unlike other sources of power they may be inclined to seek. If they can learn to use their writing skills instead of trying to intimidate or overpower their teachers and classmates, they may discover a tool they can use in situations in which power is used against them.

In the following chapters, I discuss specific ways to help young writers approach difficult issues, both directly and indirectly, through activities that can be used in a variety of classroom and other situations. I encourage you to read Part 1 before trying the activities in Part 2. The guidelines I suggest will support you as you work with your students and receive the gifts of their writing.

1

Know Yourself

In order to set up a safe writing environment for your students, you need to be clear about your own values, the authority structure you trust, and how that works within your teaching situation. If you know where you stand with your students and colleagues, and if you understand what is within your control and what is beyond it, you can communicate that to your students. The clarity you provide will create stability in your classroom, and your students will feel safe.

In this chapter, I raise a number of questions and offer advice based on what has worked for me. But I do so with great humility. I know of no job more challenging than that of a classroom teacher. If you are managing the day-to-day lesson plans, paperwork, discipline, parent conferences, faculty meetings, and possibly lunch, recess, or bus duty, and you still have time and enthusiasm enough to read this book, you should be offering me advice!

Having said that, I'll now address a few things I urge you to consider as you work with your students on their writing and encourage them to write about personal topics.

Your Relationship With Your Students

The most important thing you can do to encourage your students to write honestly and freely is to value them as people and let them know that you respect their words and experiences. If you don't genuinely value and appreciate them, and treasure their writing, nothing you do will elicit their most powerful words. If your respect is genuine, it will permeate all you do, and you will see the results in your students' work.

Different teachers show respect for their students in different ways. Your way will reflect your personality and teaching style. How much distance do you need between yourself and your students? Are you more comfortable with a formal relationship, with very clear teacher/student boundaries, or do you like to get to know your students more personally? Be honest about who you are and what you need, and work with your strengths.

A formal relationship generally gives you more control. Your students know your system and have figured out ways to work within it. But they may not feel comfortable opening up to you, in conversation or in their writing. If you want to encourage students to write about things that matter deeply to them, you may need to spend some time creating an atmosphere that makes that possible. You can do it in a formal way by creating a particular day of the week or time of day when personal writing and sharing can occur in your classroom. The atmosphere might be different during that time. You might let students move their desks around or sit in a corner of the room when they are writing. There might be a little more time for informal conversation.

You might experiment with relaxing your own authority structure during writing time. Let your students ask you one question that's not about school. You can choose whether or not to answer it. Or let someone ask a question that everyone in the class, including you, can answer or choose not to answer. These questions can be simple and nonintrusive: "What's your favorite color?" "What are you good at?" "Who or what inspires you?"

These are ways of breaking down, or at least penetrating, the barrier between students and teachers and shifting the basis for authority from a one-way teacher-to-student model to one of mutual respect. The word *authority* has *author* at its root, and you are encouraging your students to be authors. They are the authorities on their own lives. Offer them respect, whether or not they have earned it through good grades or good behavior, and see how that respect affects their writing and the atmosphere in your classroom.

If, on the other hand, you already have a fairly easygoing relationship with your students and they feel free to share their private lives with you, their writing will probably reflect that. The initial opening up will be easier, but you may need to work a little harder to require the discipline needed to achieve a polished piece of writing. Again, use what you are good at to accomplish this: talk to the students about what they need to work on, and let them help you structure the class time in such a way that everyone can complete their best writing.

Whatever your style or approach, your relationship with your students will change as the school year goes on. If you remain open—not pushy, just quietly open—the trust between you will deepen, and your students will become more able to write about whatever is most on their minds.

Your Motivation

Why are you interested in having your students write about their personal lives? Most of my own motives are good and honorable, and I assume yours are too, but it doesn't hurt to question some of the reasons we may have for encouraging our students to write about the difficult things in their lives. Usually the best motives have an element that requires some caution, and the most questionable have an honorable side. Here are a few, as I've sorted them out:

Admiration for the students' ability to face difficult situations head-on and survive to write about them: When I read about kids who are struggling with their parents' alcoholism, or the death of a sibling, or the temptation to carry a gun, or a decision about whether or not to report knowledge of a crime, I am often amazed at the strength they muster and the integrity of their decisions. I love to help them find the words to bolster their own best qualities in difficult circumstances.

But be careful, especially if your own life is relatively safe, comfortable, and prosperous, not to encourage children to write so that you can get a window into another world. And if you do look in the windows they open for you, do so with great respect. Don't be nosy.

A desire to share your skill and, thus, your power: Clear expression, spoken and written, is a source of power. Many students believe that good writing is an inherent trait, a matter of "being smart." There is great satisfaction in seeing them discover that writing is a teachable and learnable skill.

Figure 1–1   The author of "Almost Dead" (p. 103) offers this advice.

Do you have any advice for teachers who are trying to help their students write about difficult things in their lives? Its the dumbest thing because everyone says it but its true. they should be open. they should listen like your the only person alive and even if the student does not want help, always offer it.

But keep in mind how difficult the art of writing can be for many students, especially if they are trying to write about something personal. Honor them for their efforts: no matter what we do to help, they are the ones who do the courageous writing.

Compassion for people who have suffered or are suffering: Respectful and attentive reading is one way to offer compassion, and it can be comforting for a child to know that you are willing to listen and care. You may be the only adult your students confide in, and writing may be the only way they can tell the truth about some aspects of their lives. I believe that this can literally save children's lives.

But I would caution against thinking of your teaching as therapy. Don't try to get your students to reveal themselves through their writing. Allow them to use their life experience in their writing, *if they want to,* but don't ever press for more information or try to get them to write about something because you think it would be good for them to do so. It may, in fact, be helpful to them, but that is their business, not yours.

Your Levels of Energy and Compassion

There are times when I come home from teaching writing to young people feeling utterly exhausted. Young people are experiencing so much pain, and I feel like I'm standing out there, grounded, absorbing hit after hit of their hard truth like a lightning rod in a wild thunderstorm. I feel very strongly that adults should take these hits for children if we can, but I hesitate to advise anyone else to do so without offering some warning about the effect it can have on you on a very personal level.

If I present a neutral writing activity, in a "regular" classroom, where just a few students are likely to write about painful experiences, I can teach four or five classes a day. But if there is anything about the activity that specifically invites writing about violence or trauma, or if the classroom has a high percentage of students who have experienced trauma, I can't teach more than two or three classes a day, and I have to make time in each day for some unemotional activities—such as swimming or walking.

For an elementary teacher, it is possible to manage the level of emotional involvement with your students by balancing the classroom activities within any given week. You learn which children need the most attention and how you can offer that in a multitude of ways, including, but not limited to, your response to their writing.

But for middle school and high school teachers, it can be trickier. You may not be able to do these writing activities with all your students at the same time. You might want to have one class doing a research paper while another class works on writing of a more personal nature.

However you decide to proceed, think about how your own degree of commitment, level of compassion, and amount of time and energy can best fit with the needs of your students. Be as steady as you can, but be aware of your own needs, too, and how your needs may change from time to time.

I remember one situation when I had to intentionally keep myself at a distance from something a student wrote. I was ready to begin a two-week poetry residency in an elementary school when I received a phone call telling me that my father was not expected to live more than a week. Months earlier, when I scheduled the residency, I had done my best to plan around this, but the "six weeks to six months" the doctors predicted had stretched into thirteen months and I wasn't sure what to do. I had just returned from a visit with him—he was in Colorado, I was in Oregon—where we had said a tentative, but poignant, good-bye.

I decided to go ahead with the residency and interrupt it if I had to. The two weeks went smoothly, though there was a shadow over them. My delight in the children's work was actually a nice distraction. Then, on the morning of the final day of the residency, I was awakened by the phone call from my sister, telling me that Dad had passed away an hour earlier.

Could I do it? Could I put this aside and get through that last day, teaching poetry to enthusiastic third and fourth graders? There are no substitute teachers in such work, no personal leave, and it would have been very difficult to come back a week or two later and finish that one last day. I decided to teach the four classes as planned, and I thought I'd be okay as long as I didn't tell anyone what had happened.

Everything was fine until the last class of the day when one of the children asked me to read her poem to the class. I read the title out loud, "My Grandpa's Funeral," and knew I would not be able to read her poem without crying. At some other time, I might have been able to share my own experience in response to her poem, but that day, I knew what I had to do.

Any mother who has ever read *Horton Hears a Who* for the 108th time when she has a deadline the next day at work knows how to do this: I read the words with my voice but totally disengaged my mind from them. The child didn't know, I didn't cry, and twenty minutes later I was on my way to a friend's house, where I could collapse in tears over a cup of tea.

I'm not, of course, suggesting that you adopt such an attitude as a regular strategy. As a teacher of writing, it is essential that you engage with student writers and let them know that you care about them as people and as writers.

It is also good to let them know you as a whole person. But self-awareness is crucial, and a certain amount of self-protection is sometimes necessary.

Your Support System

Part of knowing yourself is knowing what you need in order to do your best work. I have found, through long and sometimes difficult experience, that I am most successful when I work with at least one supportive adult. It can be a teacher's aide, a principal, a colleague, a parent or a group of parents, a guidance counselor, or, in my work as a writer in residence, the classroom teacher who has invited me. Much of my recent work has been in collaboration with other artists (dance, percussion, visual arts, theatre) and I have seen that the benefits of artistic collaboration are enormous. However it can be arranged, I find that just having another adult in the room with me makes me feel more competent.

And yet, I need a certain degree of autonomy. I don't like someone looking over my shoulder, telling me what to do and how to do it. This may seem like a contradiction, but I almost always manage to set up a situation that gives me both support and freedom. In the rare situations when I find myself floundering, I may think the lesson plan didn't work, but in fact, it's usually a breakdown in a support system.

What about you? Do you like to work alone or with other adults? Do you establish trusting relationships fairly easily, or are you wary of working with others? Pay attention to what setup works best for you, and then do what you can to create such a situation. When your students are writing well, look beyond what you did to elicit the writing, and notice who was in the room with you and how that person may have supported you. If your students don't respond to a writing activity, think about whether you were comfortable in presenting it and, if not, what you could do to create a situation that would make you — and, as a probable result, your students — more secure.

Your Personal Experience

Be aware of your own experience with any topics you are inviting your students to explore and of how that experience will affect your reading of student work. If you are going through a difficult time yourself, it may be hard for you to read student stories; if you are a survivor of a traumatic experience, you may become more involved than you otherwise would.

Take a few minutes and try the following exercise yourself. It will help you understand what it means to your students to think, speak, and write about something extremely personal.

Read "Watermelon Hill" (p. 68) and "'The Universe Is a Safe Place for Souls'" (p. 90). Do either of these stories remind you of something that happened to you when you were the age your students are now? Think of one thing that caused you some degree of pain when you were young: someone picked on you in the locker room; you were humiliated when you refused to fight or when you tried to fight; you overreacted to a threat and hurt someone; you yelled at someone and made him cry; you think you may have been molested but you can't quite remember; you stood by and said nothing when someone was tormented; you should have done something when your friend showed you her bruises; you thought you — or your girlfriend — might be pregnant.

Start by thinking about the answers to the following questions:

- Have you ever written anything about this?
- Do you think you could?
- What would be hard about it?

Now, get out some paper and a pencil, paying attention to your feelings as you do so. Imagine that you are in a group of strangers, or a mixed group of friends and strangers, and that you are being asked to do this by someone who has power over you. Wouldn't you want to know, as students always do before they begin writing: What is going to happen to this paper? Do I have to show it to anyone?

No, you don't have to show it to anyone. Now, thinking of this one incident or situation, try to put in writing the answers to the following questions, as honestly as you can:

- What happened that led up to this?
- Where were you?
- How were you feeling before it happened?
- What happened?
- How did you respond?
- Do you think you did the right thing?
- What might you have done differently?
- Were there any consequences?
- Could there still be consequences?
- How did you feel about it at the time?
- How do you feel about it now?

These are private memories, and it can feel threatening to write them down. Now imagine that you are asked to read what you have written at a faculty meeting or to hand it over to someone who will be evaluating you in some way. Do you have some sense of what your students are entrusting to you if they write honestly about something personal and allow you to read what they have written, especially if you will grade them on it?

Before you ask your students to do any of the writing activities in this book, try each activity yourself, just to get a sense of how difficult it may be. You may also get a sense of how you could be affected emotionally by your students' writing. Quite often, something a student writes will evoke a strong, and sometimes painful, memory for the teacher who reads it; it's helpful to be prepared for that.

The self-awareness you bring to this work will give you stability, and your students will rely on that stability as a strong base for their own growth as they write their way through those tumultuous years from childhood to adulthood.

2

Make It Safe

Many students do not feel safe in school. They go through the hallways looking over their shoulders, anxious about what other students might do or say. They get into a classroom and shut down, anxious about how teachers are going to wield their power, afraid of looking stupid. They often decide it's easier not to participate at all than to risk trying, only to fail. A writing classroom often exaggerates these feelings.

What is so dangerous about honest writing? It can expose students to shame, anxiety, and fear, and it can evoke strong and surprising emotions of grief and rage. In this chapter, I discuss some of these dangers and suggest things you can do to help your students overcome them.

Shame and Ambivalence

Our culture assigns negative value to a multitude of things that students either undeniably are, or, for whatever reason, think they are: poor, fat, ugly, foreign, gay, handicapped, pregnant . . . the list goes on. And then there are the things students still feel are a cause of prejudice, no matter how hard we try to claim they are not: gender and race, with race being more emotionally charged than gender. (Though my sisters and I recall, with considerable emotion, the high school English teacher who routinely wrote G.F.A.G. across the tops of our best papers. It stood for "good for a girl," and anyone who expressed dismay about it was accused of not being able to take a joke.)

Many adults and young people in America have ambivalent feelings about race: Who should feel shame about the historical treatment of Native Americans, about slavery, and about present inequities in our society? Who actually does feel shame? How is this ambivalence expressed by different races and social classes? How are deeply ingrained perceptions and attitudes reinforced or challenged? It is important, particularly if a teacher is white and students are not, that students are neither pushed to write about racial issues nor made to feel that the topic is off-limits.

One of the most effective things a writing teacher can do to diminish the anxiety students feel about anything that marginalizes them is to share good writing that makes the students feel visible. (See Appendix A.) Most textbooks now offer culturally diverse examples of writing, and you can keep a file of writing about all different kinds of experiences. As your students write about their own life experiences, keep copies of their writing to share with future students.

In this book, Ketu Oladuwa's story "I Remember Mrs. King" (p. 88) recounts a memory of injustice and doesn't blink at naming racial prejudice for what it is. Tim Seibles' poem "Kerosene" (p. 66) offers an image of anger that includes feelings about race. And Constance García-Barrio, in "Eat Dirt" (p. 106), writes lovingly about her great-grandmother who was born into slavery. When I share such writing with a class in which most of the students are African American, there is usually intense interest, which I suspect has to do with the respectful naming of something that is so often unacknowledged, especially in school, yet remains undeniably present just below the surface.

Whether or not you teach in a culturally diverse classroom, you can do a lot to help students overcome either prejudice or ambivalence about ethnicity. Find ways to honor different races and cultures at all times of the year, not just in February. If your community has ethnic or minority newspapers, subscribe to them and keep them readily available in your classroom. Have pictures on your walls depicting minority writers, women writers, writers with disabilities.

I'm not suggesting that you become overly self-conscious about any of this, and sensitivity is essential, but don't avoid mentioning things that may be important to your students. Treat each student with respect yourself, and create a classroom atmosphere that ensures that the students respect one another.

Fear of Being Teased

Directly related to anxieties about being different is a fear of being teased by classmates. Support your students in coming to an agreement that teasing is off-limits. You can't do it for them; they have to participate. Young people develop strong defenses, for good reason, and you are asking them to dismantle those defenses and be open to one another. It may be hard for them to abide by a no-teasing policy, but it's essential that you help them implement it if your writing classroom is going to be safe.

I have one rule for my writing classes: We will do our best to make sure no one is hurt by anything that happens in this class. I speak of this in two specific ways.

First, I tell them not to write anything that could be hurtful. I mention that people, including teachers, can be hurt by writing that is intended to be all in fun. I suggest that students do not use real names in their stories, whether fiction or nonfiction, if anyone could be hurt by their doing so. (In Chapter 3, I go into further detail about specific circumstances that require more attention.)

Second, I tell them that whatever is written in this class is off-limits for any kind of teasing, both during the class writing time and outside of class. I make it clear that this isn't a teacher-imposed rule; it is a group agreement. In most circumstances, I present it, then say, "Please raise your hand if you agree to this." If I think there are one or two students who really do want to agree to it but can't quite bring themselves to raise their hands, I make it a little easier by saying, "If you don't think you can abide by that, please raise your hand." I look at each student, nodding my appreciation, then say, "That's great. It's that easy; now we have a safe place for our writing. Thanks."

If someone doesn't want to agree to it, I say, "You don't have to, and you are welcome to do the writing with us, but you won't be able to listen to anyone else's writing or read your own writing to the group." If it is presented as a genuine choice, with respect for each person's decision, it is very powerful to most kids, and they almost always agree to it. I really try not to make a power play out of it.

Once I had a student who adamantly refused to agree to this. He was a special education student who had been placed in a mainstream classroom just for my residency, and it was impossible for him to believe that he would not be teased by the other students in the class. He argued at some length that "no matter what they say now, you don't know what happens at lunch time." He wanted me to define what punishment would enforce the rule, and I insisted that the rule was self-enforcing if everyone agreed to it. Finally, the classroom teacher took him aside and said he could go back to his usual classroom and come back later in the week if he decided to abide by the agreement.

That student had a point; I have no way of knowing what goes on outside the classroom. I do, however, have a great deal of trust that students take the agreement seriously. Occasionally, someone will snicker a bit at something a classmate has written, and I issue a quiet reminder that we have agreed not to do that. That's all it takes. I am respectful of each piece of writing myself, which also creates respect among the students.

Anxiety About Writing Ability

Even when students have a lot to say and a strong desire to say it, many have monumental insecurities about their writing ability. If you know who these students are, you can speak to them privately and offer to help them write or to write down what they say until they feel more confident. This reassures them that writing is more than spelling, and it reaffirms the importance of having something to say in the first place.

If students claim not to have anything to say, assure them that they do. I say things like:

- Just relax your mind, and accept what comes to you.
- Your ideas are a gift to you and you are the only one who can offer them to the rest of us.
- Don't worry about whether your ideas are good or not, just let them come to you, and accept them for whatever they are.
- You know how in some classes, you have to think hard? See if you can think soft. Maybe even close your eyes and see if an idea slips in when you're not looking.

Figure 2–1   How often do we hear just the first part, without the "aka"?

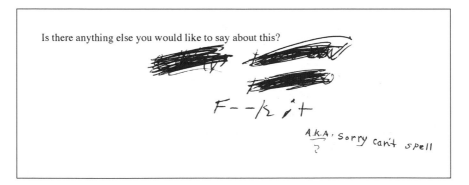

And to those students who have plenty of ideas but lack the ability to write them down, I say:

- Some people can think a lot faster than they can write. If you want someone to write down your words for you, raise your hand.
- If you know how to spell most words but not all of them, just guess at the ones you don't know and underline them. I'll come around and help you with the words you don't know, or you can use a dictionary later on.
- I'd be happy to write your poem (story) for you.

They can hardly believe this last one, but what usually happens is that they take me up on it for a sentence or two, then take the pencil out of my hand, saying they want to write the rest. If they can't write at all, I really am happy to write their words down for them.

Some students, of course, need considerable help for a long time. In such cases, help them get the support they need, so that their ability to think won't be stymied by their inability to spell and punctuate.

Offer all of this support in a matter-of-fact manner, so that the student is not embarrassed. Keep the focus on the ideas and images, praising what is wonderful in each student's thinking, whether it was actually written down by the student or by you or another adult or classmate.

Fear of Getting Bad Grades

Think about how you feel when you are being observed or evaluated. Do you use your surefire lesson plans, or do you try the riskier things that might work but could fall flat? If you want students to take risks in their writing, try to remove or minimize the pressure of grades.

For some students, the possibility of receiving a good grade is an incentive, but for many more, potential bad grades are more discouraging than they ever admit. Especially for students who have a huge "I don't care" attitude, failing grades are counterproductive. And if students are writing about something intensely personal, a bad grade on the writing can feel like a rejection of their feelings about the experience, in which case the grade becomes even more problematic.

Try to avoid passing judgment in either direction. Instead of saying, "That's good," or "That's not good," just let the student know where the writing is effective. Here are some comments that encourage writers to go on:

- I understand this part, but I'm confused here.
- I know what you mean.

- I admire your courage. It's hard to write about something like that.
- You really have a lot to say about all this, don't you?
- Wow! I never thought of that before.

This kind of support often frees students to work on spelling, punctuation, and other writing skills for their own reasons. They want to be understood, so their writing improves. The skills show up on other assignments and on standardized tests, so their grades also improve. But the focus isn't on the grade or the test score; it's on the writing.

The tricky part, of course, is that students often do their best work when they are personally invested in their writing, and it's too bad not to give them credit for that. One possibility is to give credit without giving grades, saying something like, "Keep working on this writing until it is as clear and strong as you can make it, and then you will get one hundred points for it."

I don't pretend to have all the answers about grading and evaluation; I do my own best teaching when I don't have to grade my students, and I find that students often take the most pride in their work when they are not being graded. Consider your own teaching situation, and be straightforward with your students about your grading system and how these writing activities fit into it. Then, whatever you decide about grades, do as much as you can to keep the control of the writing itself in the hands of the writer.

Strong Emotions

Writing can take people into difficult emotional terrain, and that can be frightening and surprising, both to the writer and to those who read or listen to the writing. An adult's calm presence is important at such times. Absorbing the grief or rage that young people sometimes pour forth in their writing takes a great deal of energy, but it is an essential element of creating a safe atmosphere.

CRYING

Sometimes a student starts crying when writing evokes a strong memory. It's sometimes worth mentioning that this might happen before students start writing, remaining calm about it yourself. I say, "You may be writing about an emotional event. If your writing takes you someplace you don't want to be, you can turn away from it. You can stop writing or write something different. But you don't have to. It's okay to cry, so if that happens, don't worry about it."

When someone cries, it can be a dramatic event, especially in situations where emotions are closely guarded, as they are almost all the time in most classrooms. I stay calm and speak quietly to the person. I might say, "Could I read what you're writing?" I honor either yes or no. If yes, I read and respond, briefly and compassionately, then say, "I can see that you have strong feelings about this. It's hard to write while you're crying. You might want to stop for a few minutes and just take a few deep breaths." I sometimes give the writer some tissues and a gentle touch on the back or shoulder as I move on. That is my way of acknowledging the emotion without calling too much attention to it. Usually, writers want to continue writing after a few minutes, but if they choose to stop and write about something else, let them know that you understand why they made that choice, and help them get started on something new.

Occasionally, something I read in class or something a student reads out loud makes me choke up myself, or even cry. I try to avoid it, but when it happens, it's not a problem. If I'm reading, I just stop for a minute, and then either finish or say, "Maybe someone else could finish reading this." I suspect that the writer appreciates the sympathy, and the other students are impressed with the writer for making the teacher cry!

EXPRESSIONS OF RAGE

Writing can also evoke feelings of extreme anger. I have learned to trust that such rage is usually an understandable response to something the student has experienced, perhaps at a time when it was unsafe to display any anger about the situation. Try to be strong, calm, and sympathetic, and point out that writing is a safe way to express such feelings.

Once, at a facility for kids who had been removed from their homes, a girl read a poem about being gang-raped while her father stood by laughing. A few minutes later, everyone was writing with considerable intensity, and a staff member quietly approached me and said, "We have a problem over here." I went over to the boy she indicated and saw that he had filled an entire notebook page with one word, which he was still writing over and over on the blackened paper. I watched carefully and saw that the word was *KILL*.

"What are you thinking about as you write that?" I asked, very gently.

"My father."

"What made you think of your father?"

"Sandra's poem. My father was like that with all us kids. He's under a restraining order now, and he can't have any contact with us until we're eighteen."

"So you feel safe right now?"

"I guess."

"Are you finished with this paper?" (He had stopped writing.)

"Yes."

"Here's a new piece of paper. Do you want to try to write a poem today?"

"Yes. I want to tell the truth about my father."

We stayed late that day, as a number of the kids were unusually emotional. They all read their poems and seemed to take comfort in sharing their stories. The following week, this boy was particularly gentle. He made a point of thanking me and saying good-bye. I was glad to hear that he had been placed in a safe foster home.

You will never be able to guarantee that your writing classroom is completely safe. Writing involves risk-taking, and that is part of its value. But you can be aware of the risks and do your best to minimize them so that your students will feel secure enough to take some chances in their writing.

3

Legal and Ethical Concerns

The legal system differs from state to state and from county to county. School policies differ from one district to another and sometimes from school to school within a district. You should know how all of the different systems of authority define your responsibility, and you should know the counseling resources available to your students.

It is sometimes hard to know when to be concerned, but if you are trusted with information that suggests someone is in danger or presents a danger to others, know how to get help. In the following sections, I address issues that present legal and ethical questions. Although many of these issues are inter-related, I will consider them one at a time.

Child Abuse or Neglect

In most states, you have a responsibility to report, but *not* to investigate, anything that gives you cause to suspect that a child is being abused or neglected. You should know the law and the appropriate person and agency to whom you must report.

But it's never easy to decide whether to file such a report, and the repercussions of being either right or wrong can be enormous: false accusations can damage an entire family, as well as your own reputation and your relationship with a student's parents, while unreported abuse or neglect can lead to serious injury or death. I strongly advise that you take advantage of your

17

school's support staff in any situation in which you think a child may be in danger. A principal, an assistant principal, or a guidance counselor is likely to have more knowledge and experience in dealing with such a situation than you do and may be able to put a student's writing into a larger context than you can.

It's important to be clear about this with your students. Tell them before they begin writing that if they write something that makes you think they are in any kind of danger, you will talk to a school counselor about it. Having said that makes it easier to act when you deem it necessary. If students write about abuse or neglect knowing that you'll take it seriously, it's fair to interpret their writing as a cry for help.

I approach such a situation very carefully. A conversation with a writer who has written something suggesting sexual abuse might go something like this:

"Could I talk to you privately about your story?" (I do this discreetly, moving well out of earshot of other students.) "I wasn't sure, when I read this, if the speaker in the story was a real person, but your writing made me feel like she's real, and I'm concerned about her."

"It's not true. It's not about me. I don't want to talk about it."

"Okay. I just wanted to check." (Pause; leave an opening.)

"It's about a girl I used to know. Her dad used to beat her all the time."

"All the time, or just when he was drinking?"

"Yeah . . . drinking."

"I had a friend like that, too. She really liked her dad when he was sober, but when he drank, it was like he was a different person."

"Did he just beat her, or did he, you know . . . ?"

"Sometimes he came in her room when her mom wasn't there."

"That's what my d—my friend's dad does."

"Has your friend talked to an adult about this?"

"No."

"Could I show your story to (specific name, probably a guidance counselor) and ask her to talk to you about it?"

"I guess. It's not about me."

"You're brave to write about it. The details you used really made me care about this girl."

I would follow up on the conversation by speaking to the guidance counselor or, if there were no guidance counselor, to the principal or another trusted colleague. I would be aware that the writer might seek another opportunity to speak to me privately, and I would try to be available to her, but if she didn't initiate another conversation, I probably wouldn't push it much beyond this. If something similar came up in another piece of writing, I would talk to the student again. I would remain alert but careful about drawing hasty conclusions. If my questions became more serious suspicions, I would check to see if the guidance counselor had filed a report, as required by law in my state. If not, I would do so myself.

Suicide

I take any suggestion of suicide seriously. If the subject comes up in fiction, nonfiction, drama, or poetry, or in any conversation about a student's writing, I read and listen very carefully and usually ask the student directly, "Is this something you have ever considered doing?" I've received responses ranging from "No way!" to "I used to think about it, but I don't anymore," to "I'm trying to decide."

Sometimes students are toying with the *idea* of suicide, finding it interesting to think, talk, and write about death. I don't give too much attention to that, but I'm hesitant to ignore it altogether. If I ask, "Where did you get the idea for this part of your story," and a student says, "I just put that in to make the story more exciting," I make a careful judgment call as to whether that seems likely to be true. If there has been one suicide in a community of students, pay close attention to how other students are writing about it; one suicide can lead to others.

Alyssa's story "Almost Dead" (p. 103) is an example of a way in which a student might write about suicide. I spoke to her about it, and I believed her when she told me it wasn't something she was thinking about anymore. I guessed that it was something she had dealt with in the past and that it was helpful to her to write about it. I was a visiting writer in Alyssa's classroom, and I told her teacher I had spoken with her, but I didn't pursue it beyond that.

If a student is writing in the present tense, with particular details about a means of death or imagining someone else's reaction to his or her death, I look more closely. Scott's poem gave me cause for concern:

My Life

The grass is no longer green
the roses have all died out.
I am so angry I need to shout.
I am not really afraid to die.

It's just everyone would look at me and wonder why.
Why would I take my life
with that bloody knife?
My mom would have to be mighty;
to keep busy, she would keep things very tightly.
She would be a wreck.
She would have to quit at Ivy Tech.
She would be shaky.
She would not be able to see because of the tears in her eyes.
It would be better if I just didn't die.

I asked Scott, an eighth grader, if I could show the poem to the school counselor, and he said he didn't think it was necessary, but I could if I wanted to. I did, and I felt better knowing that someone else was aware that these thoughts had crossed his mind.

I have, on occasion, felt that a student is actually suicidal, and if conversation supports this concern, I don't ask permission; I tell the student that I'm very concerned, and I need to show the writing to someone else. I don't let it drop.

Once, I had a fairly lengthy conversation with a girl who wrote that she was "trying to decide." She gestured as she spoke, saying that her father was on one side (she dropped one hand) because it would make him happy if she died, but her dog was on the other side (she raised her other hand), because who would feed him? She wasn't sure which side her sister and mother were on. She thought she might cut her wrists, and she showed me scars from where she had tried it before.

In that situation, the danger seemed clear and present. I spoke to the person in charge of the group of girls I was working with. This was not in a school, and the person I spoke to was not a professional counselor. He responded, "Oh, she always talks like that. She's just trying to get attention." I kept making phone calls until I spoke to someone who paid attention and got immediate help (the girl was hospitalized and did, in fact, attempt suicide the following week).

In general, if a student is considering suicide and writes something about it, there is a strong likelihood that the writing is a call for help and your intervention will be welcomed as a sign of concern. Doing too much is not likely to do much harm, while doing too little or doing nothing could have terribly serious and irreparable consequences. Parents certainly have a right to know about such writing and — again, with the help of a guidance counselor — may be able to help you gauge the appropriate level of concern.

Knowledge of Illegal Activity

Your students may have knowledge of illegal activities, and this can come up in their writing. On several occasions, I have held in my hand what could be interpreted as a signed confession. On other occasions, student writing suggests that a child is the victim of a crime and may not even realize it; this is often the case with teenage girls writing about rape or sexual assault.

Find out whether the law in your community requires that you report any evidence of illegal activity to the police and whether your school policy requires that you report it to school authorities. Find out whether student writing could be subpoenaed in a court case or whether you could be called as a witness. The rules may be different if the activity has occurred on school grounds, or as part of a school function, than if it occurred elsewhere. Know your responsibility to the parents of a minor, if that is defined by school policy. If not, define it for yourself.

Again, the point is to be straightforward about this with the students before you invite any writing that might venture into such territory. But don't think you need to address it in every situation; it is probably unnecessary, and could be frightening, for most elementary-age students. I don't raise this issue unless I have some reason to believe it's likely to come up.

Before I began the project that specifically invited writing about violence, I called my county prosecutor's office, and I was told that I did not have a legal responsibility to report anything the students wrote about illegal activity. While I was glad to know that I did not *have* to come forward with such information, I did not want to find myself wondering whether I *should* do so. See the scene between Ginger and Rose (p. 114) for a dramatization of the kind of dilemma this can present to students and adults.

For that reason, whatever my legal responsibilities, I tell students that I don't want to have such information. I ask them to protect themselves and me by not writing directly about anything that could get themselves or anyone else in trouble with the law. Fiction can be a safe way to write about such things, and anonymous writing might provide enough protection for you and the writer. But even fiction or anonymity may not be enough; decide whether or not you want to allow such subjects at all.

I have found that once the floodgates are open and students learn that they can write about whatever is most on their minds, a need for confession often arises. You may have students who feel guilty about something they have done or who have knowledge of a crime and are wrestling with difficult ethical decisions regarding their responsibilities to friends, family, and others. They may need to talk to someone who can counsel them in a nonjudgmental way, and their writing may be a way of seeking that help.

Clergy and lawyers have privileges of confidentiality, as well as having knowledge and experience that most teachers do not possess. I have sought out several members of the clergy in my community, diverse in terms of religious background, gender, and race, and asked them if they would be willing to counsel young people who don't have a religious affiliation of their own. You may not be able to give out specific names of clergy members, but if you have reason to believe such information is needed, you can make a general statement such as, "Lawyers and members of the clergy can talk to you without having to report what you say to the courts. You have to let them know, however, that you are talking to them as a lawyer or a clergyperson."

Again, the most important point is not to surprise your students. Don't encourage total honesty in writing and then use the writing in a way that could cause consequences that the writer did not anticipate.

Violent Fantasies

Kids have always sought to shock their elders and one another. It's fun to change the words of "Deck the Halls with Boughs of Holly" to "Deck the halls with gasoline / fa la la la la la la la la / Light a match and watch it gleam / fa la la la la la la la la / Watch the school burn down to ashes / fa la la la la la la la la / Aren't you glad you played with matches? / fa la la la la la la la laaaaa!" Adults have always known that children who sing such songs have no serious intention of burning down their school.

But then came Columbine and other terrifying events of school violence. People were shocked after the Columbine shootings to discover that the students who shot their classmates had planned the day in considerable detail, in writing and on videotape, and that teachers had seen some of these plans before they were carried out. In retrospect, it was hard to imagine how something so blatantly violent could have been ignored; but retrospect is always clearer than foresight. In any case, it became apparent that what had previously been unimaginable was now within the realm of imagination. Teachers everywhere became more cautious.

Later that year, a student was suspended from a different school for his response to a Halloween homework assignment: "Write about something frightening." He imagined, in a fictional story, someone being attacked and killed, and when his writing was interpreted as "violent fantasy," he was suspended from school. Again, a cry of public outrage arose, but this time for the opposite reason: "This student was suspended for doing his homework!"

Teachers walk a tightrope on the question of what to do about violent fantasies in student writing, and again, our decisions can have serious consequences. I don't pretend to have a definitive answer, but I would advise that you think the questions through before a difficult situation arises. Know your school policy; know your own feelings; and be sure that your students know where you stand. In general, I would offer this advice:

- The more specific the fantasy, the greater the cause for concern. If any person is named as the object of a violent fantasy, pay particular attention.
- Make a clear distinction between writing about violence in a thoughtful manner and writing violent scenes or lyrics because they are exciting.
- If you have cause for concern, speak to the student and ask direct questions about the intent of the writing. Keep a level head and even a sense of humor. If someone says, "I was just kidding around," point out that something intended to be humorous can sometimes be scary or hurtful. Give the writer a chance to apologize.
- An ongoing, repeated, or obsessive fantasy should be taken seriously.
- Be sure that your concern and attention are given to the writer as well as to anyone who feels threatened by the writing.
- Keep parents and guidance counselors informed of any concern.

Censorship

This is not an entirely separate category from the previous discussion, but questions can come up about language and subject matter other than violence. A fourth grader may delight her classmates by using the word *poop* in a poem, and a ninth grader may want to write rap lyrics that have the word *bitch* or *nigger* (or *nigga*) in every other line.

Think this through before it arises as a specific incident. Does your school have a policy about censorship versus freedom of expression? Do you agree with it? If not, would you be willing to challenge it? Find out if this question has come up in the past, and discuss it with your students so that they know the limits of what is allowed. Then be honest about your own sensibilities. Here, rather than guidelines, I have two stories:

When Ryan, a sixth grader, wrote a poem including the image of "a fart in an empty cave" the class erupted in laughter and looked to me to see if I would express disapproval. I just smiled and acknowledged that it was a vivid image. The next week when I passed back the poems, I asked if anyone remembered Ryan's poem. Everyone remembered the fart, but no one remembered anything else about the poem. I asked Ryan if that was what he wanted, and he gave it some thought and decided that he really wanted the poem to be more than a joke. As much as possible, I try to keep the focus on the actual effect of the words.

Another time, when teaching poetry in a nonschool setting, I received a batch of poems from teenage boys that contained a lot of language that was disrespectful of women. I discussed it with my coworkers and we decided, though not without some discomfort, that we wanted to meet these young men where they were, rather than set rules about what language they could use.

But when I sat down to type their poems, I found I could not give them the respect that careful typing requires. I typed them up but left out the lines I found offensive. When I returned the poems, I said, "Some of you will notice that your poems aren't typed up exactly the way you wrote them. I'm sorry. I know women and girls who have been badly hurt by the kind of language you are using, and I just can't bring myself to type it."

I was not exactly making a rule; I was being honest about my response, and they heard that. After a quiet pause, one of the boys said, "You know what, I agree with her. I don't like that kind of language either." A few others murmured assent, and no one really seemed to mind. Where I had expected a mild confrontation, I found instead a meeting point.

In most schools, such a question would not even get that far. Your school probably has a clear policy about the use of offensive language, and your students will know what words are off-limits. Again, it's better to be clear about this from the start than to wait until it comes up and then impose consequences.

Beyond the question of offensive language, there are complex questions about freedom to express ideas that may offend others; there are boundaries to be set regarding stories of a sexual nature. How you handle these issues will be particular to your own sensibilities, the maturity of your students, and the degree of support from your colleagues and community.

As in all your work with students, I urge you to be as direct and honest as you can about the questions that arise around issues of censorship and freedom of expression. Students are trying out their voices, and freedom is essential, but they also need to learn that their words have an effect on others. Help them learn how to write in clear, strong language and try to respect their truth even if it is different from your own. You may learn to see what they mean underneath a sometimes crude surface; they may discover that "respectable" language can be stronger than "offensive" language.

I've covered a lot of ground in this chapter. I don't want to leave the impression that you need to go through all these points, one by one, before each writing assignment. Rather, give them some thought and address them as you see a need to do so. The guidelines I've put forward here are really just an extension of the guidelines regarding safety and respect.

One final thought: In responding to your students' personal problems, I encourage you to rely on the support systems available to you in your school and community, but you may also wish to consult the following websites, which offer useful information, advice, and links to other related sites:

Center for Disease Control and Prevention (CDC): Youth Violence and Suicide Prevention Team: <http://www.cdc.gov/ncipc/dvp/yvpt/yvpt.htm>

Youth Crisis and Information Hotlines: <http://www.sanpedro.com/spyc/hotline.htm>

4

Presenting Writing
Activities to Students

I taught for three years in a one-teacher school in Alaska in a small community where all the children in my class were siblings or cousins to one another. Every Wednesday morning was writing time and I had to do little more than say, "It's Wednesday," to get everyone writing stories, poems, letters, and essays. Since it was a multigrade classroom, any activity had to be adaptable to many different levels of reading and writing ability.

In that situation, I learned to keep all the writing activities both flexible and simple: "Everyone choose a picture and write a story about it," or "Let's write a letter to our favorite mushers, wishing them luck in the Iditarod," or "Interview people who remember when the first airplane landed, and write down what they tell you."

Later, teaching fifth grade in a somewhat larger community, I kept that tradition of regular writing time and initiated a few slightly more ambitious writing projects: an oral history of our school (the oldest elementary school still in use in Alaska), a class anthology of student stories and poems, a collection of writing entitled *Stories of Love and Courage*.

In my work as a writer in residence, and in much of my violence prevention work, I often have only four or five short sessions with student writers. In such work, I usually present a series of writing activities that will ensure success to young, often reluctant writers when they have limited time for polishing and revising.

When I was asked to contribute to a large-scale project in the high schools of my community, helping young people write about their experiences with violence for the purpose of writing a play, the work was short-term in each school, but it was carefully planned and executed as part of the larger project. The students knew they were part of an endeavor with a very particular purpose: to dramatize the effect of violence on young people in our community.

In this section, I offer guidelines to help you present a wide range of writing activities, in a variety of situations, with an emphasis on encouraging and responding to writing of a personal nature.

The writing activities vary in their degree of neutrality. That is, many of the activities are *not* designed to elicit particularly emotional or personal writing. These are generally the best for short-term writing activities. You can use them without getting permission from students' parents and without the necessity of laying a lot of groundwork. Students may still respond to them with personal writing, but you will not be asking them to do so.

Most of your writing activities should be fairly neutral. Don't assume that because your students have serious problems, or a lot of experience with violence, for example, that that is all they want to write about. Give them opportunities to be as honest as they want to be, and accept their honesty within whatever limits you need to set (as discussed in Chapters 2 and 3), but be careful about directly asking them to write about something personal.

In particular, be very careful about making any suggestions as to what topic a particular student might choose. If you say, "Corinne, why don't you write about having a baby when you were in eighth grade," Corinne might well resent your bringing that up for a number of reasons:

- She is not ready to write about it, so she becomes defensive.
- Not too many people know about it, and she'd like to keep it that way.
- Everyone knows about it, and she feels like that's all they know about her.
- She's tired of thinking about her baby and wants to think about going to college.

You never really know what is most on your students' minds. I remember one evening when I was working with fifteen- to eighteen-year-old boys in a court-ordered violence-prevention program. It was several weeks into the program, and they had done a lot of talking and writing about guns, drugs, difficulties with parents and girlfriends, and hard decisions about gang affiliation. I had assessed their interests and printed out poems on various subjects, which I'd left lying on a table, saying, "When you finish writing your poem, you can go to the table and look through the poems I brought in and take home any that you like."

I'd included poems by contemporary African American and Hispanic poets about the streets and about prison, and I thought those would be the most popular. But I'd also noted an interest in love poems — they were teenagers, after all — and had included several of Shakespeare's love sonnets. When a mild melee broke out around the table, I went over to investigate and discovered that it was the sonnets they were fighting over. I made a list of who wanted which poems, promising to bring in extra copies the following week.

You never know what activities will allow your students to speak their own most important truths, and it's not a good idea to try to guess in advance what those truths might be. But if you provide a multitude of opportunities in a welcoming and respectful atmosphere, your students will find the support they need in order to do their best writing, saying whatever they are ready to say.

Defining the Project

Begin by defining the exact nature of the writing project. How much time will you have together, and how much can be devoted to this particular project? Give your students a rough idea of how your time will be used.

What is the purpose of the writing? Are you planning to write a class play? Will you be putting together a collection of poems and stories? Who will see it? Having a larger purpose than a single assignment often inspires students to write more openly and courageously and to take greater care with their work. You might put together a collection of stories just for yourselves and make copies for parents and other teachers and one for the school library. Or each student could create an individual book.

While it is rarely realistic for an individual student or class to set out to write a book that will be published by a "real" publisher, there are businesses that will publish a very professional-looking volume for a reasonable cost (see Appendix A). Set a goal that is possible for your students to reach. Don't underestimate their ability to write and to learn, but don't set a goal that depends on the decisions of unknown publishers or on an extraordinary amount of luck or knowledge of the world of publishing, either.

Explore the possibilities with your class and figure out what resources are available to you. Then, with either a short-term or a long-term goal in mind, answer any questions the students may have about the purpose of the activity, taking time to respond seriously to each question.

If you intend to specifically and directly address any sensitive topics, send a note home to let parents know what you will be doing and why, explaining clearly how the student writing will be used.

Getting Started

Ask students to clear their desks except for two sheets of paper and something to write with. If you do that before you begin, the rest of the writing time can be relatively free of interruptions.

For each activity in this book, I suggest examples of writing to use as an introduction. If you would like to use any of the writing examples in this book, you can read them aloud to your class or create your own overheads or handouts based on the work to use with your students. Or, you may prefer to use your students' work as examples. If so, each time you do an activity, save several student examples to share with future classes—with permission of the writer, of course. The examples serve both as models for the activity and as starting points to help students think of things to write about. Examples of writing about difficult topics can also be a way to give students permission to approach those topics in their own writing.

Some of the activities suggest that you do a group activity before doing individual writing. That often relaxes students and eases them into participation.

For many students, deciding what to write about is a big stumbling block. Their indecision usually indicates not a lack of ideas, but a lack of confidence. So, in each activity, after you have explained what you are doing and have presented the examples, but before you give the specific writing prompts, make sure that each student has an idea. This will prevent the scenario of two or three students not writing anything and then, when the class is over, saying, "I couldn't think of anything to write about."

In some of the poetry activities, the writing itself generates the idea, so students don't have to think of what to write about before they begin. But in the nonfiction, fiction, and drama activities, it's best for students to begin with some idea of where they're going, even if they eventually end up going somewhere else.

Here are a few steps you can take to help students find ideas:

Ask everyone to think of an idea within the parameters of the particular writing activity. Make a few suggestions, then pause for about a minute while they are thinking and answer any questions they ask regarding what is okay to write about.

Then say, "Put your finger in the air if you are still thinking, and put it down once you know what you are going to write about." This is subtly different than asking, "How many people are still thinking?" and having them raise their hands to affirm that. To many students, a raised hand indicates participation, but if you begin with everyone's hand up, then *not* having your hand up connotes participation, so as soon as hands start going down, everyone gets the idea that everyone else is participating. Not only that, but

Figure 4–1   Students raise their hands until they decide what to write about.

the reluctant students may start to think, "Everyone else has an idea and I don't, so I'd better think fast."

Wait quietly for a minute or two. The quiet is important, as it indicates a respect for the time it takes to think, without the teacher talking. When most hands are down, say, "Great, almost everyone has an idea. Just wait a minute for these last three people to think of something. It's okay for them to take their time." But of course, they don't want to take their time, with the whole class waiting for them, so they almost always come up with something. If, after two or three minutes, a few students still don't have an idea, go to them and quietly ask a few questions that may suggest a possible idea.

For example:

"What are you thinking about?"

"Nothing."

"What are you interested in?"

"Nothing."

"Are you in any sports?" (or other leading questions, such as "Do you have any pets?" "Have you ever been in a fight?" "Has anyone ever treated you unfairly?")

"Yeah." (It usually takes a few questions to get to that first reluctant "yeah.")

"Which sport do you like best?"

"Basketball."

"That's not usually a violent sport. How are conflicts solved in basketball, without resorting to violence?" (if, for example, the activity involves writing about violence).

"Well, you should have seen this one time . . . "

The student starts talking about "this one time" and after about a minute, you can point out that what you've just heard would be about a page of writing. This seems to amaze and encourage reluctant writers; maybe it is the discovery that the story already exists, and all they have to do is write it down.

Once everyone has an idea of what to write about, lead a guided writing exercise, as suggested in the chapters about specific writing activities. You can hand out a worksheet or read or speak prompts out loud. Emphasize that this is a prewriting or warm-up activity (if that's what it is, of course; some of the quick-take activities don't require prewriting). Then ask the students to create a silence (a more active and positive request than "Be quiet!") so everyone can work quietly and independently for a few minutes.

Helping Students as They Are Writing

Circulate among the students, looking at the papers to see if everyone is writing. If someone isn't writing, pause to talk about whatever may be a sticking point. Some students may have started with an idea and abandoned it, and you'll need to continue the kind of conversation suggested earlier to help them get a new idea or to encourage them to continue with the abandoned one.

If a student says even a few words, that's a starting point. If you think it will be helpful, write down those first few words — or phrases or whole sentences — as the student is talking, then hand the pencil back and let the writer continue.

Scan the class for raised hands, and offer help as needed. If someone raises a question that you think other students may also be wondering about, interrupt briefly to say, "Oh, yes, this is something I meant to tell all of you . . . "

Just glance at what students are doing, but don't read over anyone's shoulder without permission. A simple "Can I see what you're working on?" is enough, giving respect to the response, whether yes or no or not yet. If you are given permission to read a work in progress, your comments should be quiet and encouraging: "I love this!" or "Tell me more here." If something is unclear, point that out in a matter-of-fact manner. Your comments should suggest that you are really interested and you want to understand.

Figure 4–2   Circulate and talk to students as they are working.

If you see a great example of something you're teaching or of something that you forgot to mention, it's okay to interrupt the rest of the class once or twice to share the good example, with the writer's permission.

Bringing the Writing Activity to a Close

If the writing activity is neutral (not specifically inviting writing about personal topics), you can bring it to a fairly quick close, giving students an opportunity to share their writing and briefly acknowledging something noteworthy in each piece. If, however, the students have delved into topics that are likely to have brought up troublesome feelings for them, be sure to leave time for adequate closure.

As you near the end of your writing time, especially if you are teaching middle school or high school, where the students will be going on to another class, pause, with your eye on the clock. It is important not to have the class bell ring and everyone leave with their minds in the middle of a difficult scene. If there is time for discussion, ask if students want to share or talk about their writing. Remind everyone of the agreement not to tease or make fun of anyone in any way, in or out of the classroom. Some students will want to read what they have written, and others may have questions or advice or encouragement for them. If questions are addressed to you, respond briefly, and see if it's possible to engage other students in response to them.

Collect the papers, telling the class when you expect to return them and what they should expect from you in response. If you can truthfully make such a distinction, let them know that you will not "correct" these papers but will make comments to help them develop their writing.

Thank them for the hard work they have done, and say something like, "You may be writing about something emotional, and I don't want you to leave the room feeling disturbed about that. Sometimes when you are writing about something difficult, it's helpful to stop and take a deep breath and then let it out slowly. Let's do that together. Imagine that any grief or hurt is gathered into your breath and then carried out with it. See if you can leave in a peaceful mood."

The students may or may not actually take the deep breath and let it out, but the important thing is to acknowledge that you have gone into territory a little unusual for school and to help them go on to their next class without carrying the emotions generated by this writing, which for some of the students may have been surprising and strong.

5

Helping Students Develop
Their Writing

For most of the writing activities I suggest, you will need time outside of class to respond adequately to student writing. Plan your time, and know your own needs and limitations. If you are a high school or middle school teacher, you may not be able to do this kind of writing with all your classes at the same time.

Eventually, students can learn to respond helpfully to their classmates' writing, but initially, most response will come from the teacher. Here are a few things you can do to help students get the most from your comments.

Responding to First Drafts

Read papers with a pencil and a yellow highlighter in your hand. Use the highlighter generously to draw attention to good examples of whatever you have emphasized in class and to anything that interests you for any other reason. The highlighted passages don't have to be perfectly constructed or correctly spelled. You are looking for concrete details that flesh out the writing, but instead of writing, "Be more specific," at each vague passage, you are calling attention to each place where the writer does use specific detail.

For written comments, a pencil is more humble than a pen. As you read through a paper, you may change your mind about one of your comments, and a pencil allows you to alter or delete it. Students often have an especially negative response to red ink and have a hard time reading red comments constructively. They often joke about their papers "bleeding," and I suspect that beneath the joking surface of these comments, there is some truth about how red ink makes them feel.

An introductory writing exercise usually doesn't produce a finished piece of writing, but you will get a sense of where the writing is going. You can pencil in a suggested frame for a story or make a suggestion about a possible form for a poem, or you can just express an interest and ask a question or two to draw the writing out.

At this point, it's not very useful to call attention to misspellings or problems with sentence structure or punctuation unless they prevent you from understanding what the writer is trying to say. Comments and notations should be designed to explore the nuances of the writing and give the writer an idea of how to develop it.

Figure 5–1 First draft of "Pain" (p. 84): Call attention to what is effective and suggest a possible structure.

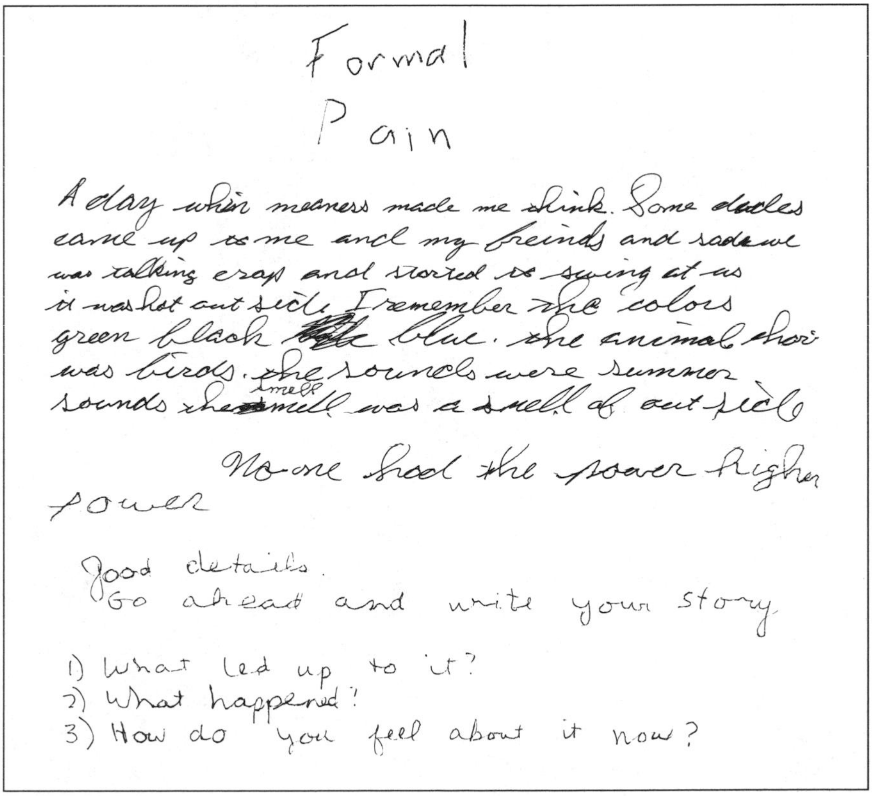
Formal

Pain

A day when meaness made me shink. Some dudes came up to me and my freinds and sade we was talking crap and started to swing at us it was hot out side I remember the colors green black ~~the~~ blue. the animal thar was birds. the sounds were summer sounds the smell was a smell of out side

No-one had the power higher power

Good details.
Go ahead and write your story.

1) What led up to it?
2) What happened?
3) How do you feel about it now?

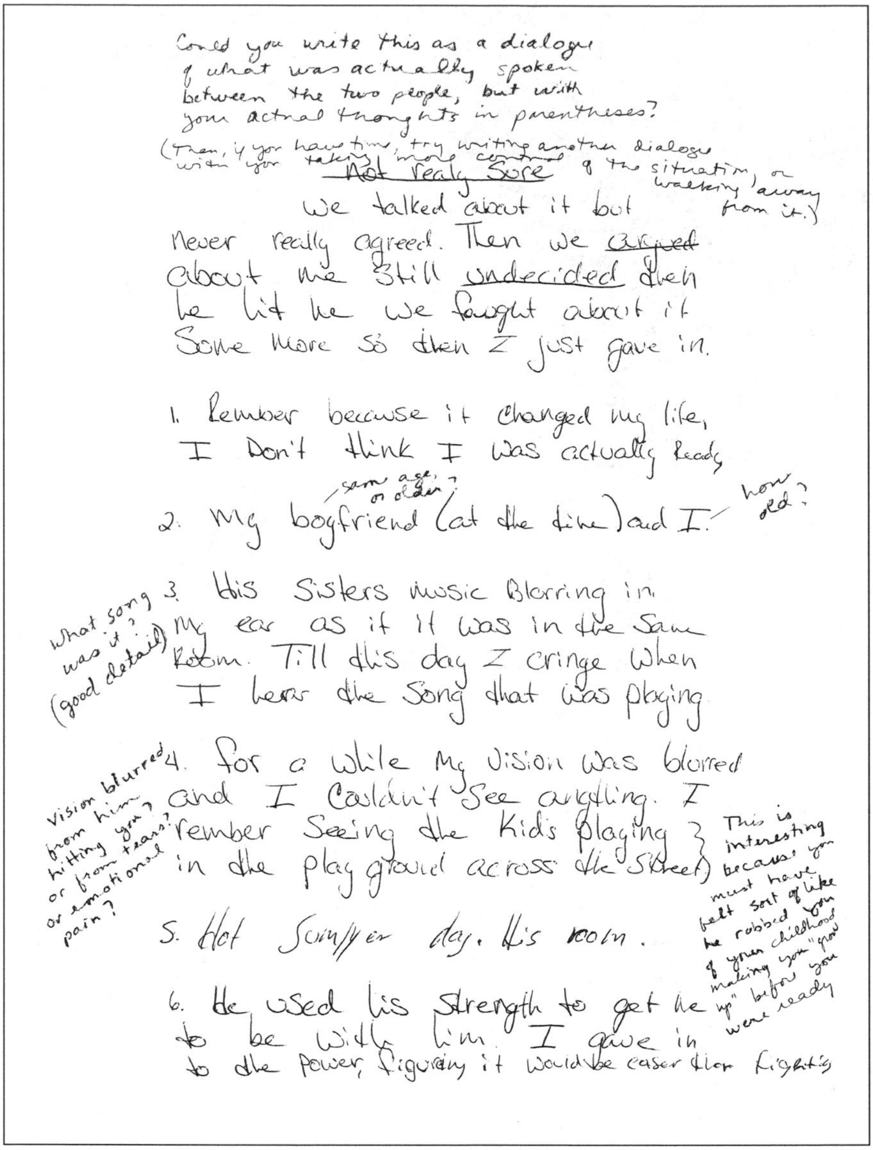

Could you write this as a dialogue
of what was actually spoken
between the two people, but with
your actual thoughts in parentheses?

(Then, if you have time, try writing another dialogue
with you taking more control of the situation, or
walking away
from it.)

Not realy Sore

We talked about it but
never really agreed. Then we argued
about me Still undecided then
he lit he we fought about it
Some More so then I just gave in.

1. Remember because it changed my life,
   I Don't think I was actually ready

2. My boyfriend (at the time) and I
   sam age or older?   how old?

3. His Sisters music Blarring in
   my ear as if it was in the Same
   Room. Till this day I cringe when
   I hear the song that was playing
   what song was it? (good detail)

4. for a while My Vision was blorred
   and I Couldn't See anything. I
   rember Seeing the Kids Playing
   in the play ground across the Street
   vision blurred from him hitting you? from tears? or from emotional pain?
   This is interesting because you must have felt sort of like he robbed you of your childhood making you "grow up" before you were ready

5. Hot Summer day. His room.

6. He used his Strength to get me up
   to be with him. I gave in
   to the power, figuring it would be easier than fighting

Figure 5–2   First draft of "Bob and Jan" (p. 113): Sometimes you'll want to respond to the personal content of a first draft.

7. I was afraid of many things
I was afraid of losing him, I
was afraid he would hurt he.
I tried not to let my fear show,
make my self look like I was okay
with it

8. I feel like I still could
not stand up to him now.

9. if someone else would have
been thier it would not have happened
at that time, but I dlink it probably
would have happened.

     I want to give you some support
on this. You have an absolute right to
decide what is good for you in every situation
This is too high a price to pay for keeping
a boyfriend, and if he doesn't agree, then
he's not worth keeping. It might help to
think about the possibility that you could
get pregnant. You have a right to choose
a kind father for your children and to wait
until you're both ready to be good parents together

As you focus on the writing, remain aware that this is a real person sharing real emotions. Sometimes it is appropriate to express concern or compassion; sometimes you really can't help offering advice of a personal nature!

If a story raises any concern about the writer's safety, or if you think it may be a call for help, flag it with a particular color of sticky note. Then, when you have passed back the papers and the students are working on revisions, you can look for those flags as you walk around the class and unobtrusively stop to speak with individual students about your concerns.

Similarly, if you think a brief lesson on a mechanical aspect of writing will be useful, put a different colored flag on that, with a note telling the student that you want to offer some help with paragraphs, verb agreement, or punctuation. Students are usually receptive to a particular pointer when it is presented not as a way to correct a mistake, but as a way of making a specific piece of writing more effective.

I remember one instance when a section of dialogue in a student's story was nearly impossible to decipher. It would have taken me a long time to edit the paper, pointing out how to fix each mistake, so I put a sticky note on that section of the story and wrote, "Ask me how to punctuate this." Then, as I went around the room, I stopped and spent about five minutes with the student, showing him how to start a new line for each speaker, and what punctuation to use.

A flash of recognition crossed his face, and he got out his literature textbook, turned to a story, and exclaimed, "Like this, right?" He then proceeded to look back and forth from the textbook to his story, and when he finished, his story was easy to read. On his evaluation of the class, when asked, "What did you gain from this writing experience?" he wrote, "Learned to punctuate." He clearly knew how to find the information he needed but had apparently never had reason to apply it before.

I also use sticky notes as a way to give quick encouragement. I may be really pressed for time, but I can usually manage to write an inch and a half by two inches of *something* on each paper, and if I'm not quite so busy, maybe even three by three! I think students like those notes because they don't mess up their papers. I write things like:

- I love your first sentence!
- Good details here.
- Great ending!
- This is really sad.
- Thank you for this beautiful poem.

First Rewrite

After you have made your written comments, and before you return the papers to the class, discuss all the writing in a general way, thanking all the students for their spectacular beginnings and pointing out the things you especially appreciated. This serves as a review and it focuses attention and boosts confidence. With permission from the writers, read a few passages from five or six of the papers, pointing out specific things the students have done well.

Don't return the writing until you have told the students what they will be doing that day, because once they have their papers with your responses, they will be eager to start writing and less interested in listening to you address the whole class. This is a good time to offer instruction about structure, point of view, and other details specific to genre. (For specific suggestions about writing in different genres, see Part 3 and Appendix A.)

When you have given your comments and instructions, pass back the students' papers, telling them not to take off your flags. Ask them to clear their desks and create a silence so that everyone can concentrate. They should each get out a clean piece of paper and either continue the work they started earlier or revise according to your comments. As they are working, circulate among them, quietly responding to questions and encouraging anyone who is having a hard time. Make a point of speaking with the students whose writing you have flagged. If there is any possibility that an overheard conversation could embarrass a student, move to a more private place so you can speak more freely.

About ten minutes before the class is over, invite the students to read their work. Usually several people are happy to do this. Remind the class of the agreement to respect each person's writing. Generally, the writing is received with rapt attention; the students are amazed at themselves and one another for having experienced these things and for being able to write about them.

Occasionally, no one volunteers to read. If that happens, use other means of sharing the stories.

Safe Ways of Sharing

- Trade papers with one friend and read silently.
- Divide into small groups and read stories aloud to the group.
- Give the story to a friend and ask the friend to read it anonymously to the class.

If you let them do any of these things, be sure the sharing is still voluntary for each writer. Remember, control of the writing should remain in the hands of the writer.

But it's best if at least some of the writing can be shared with the entire class so that you can offer encouraging responses for everyone to hear and so

Figure 5-3   A student reads her work to the class.

that trust continues to be built among the class members. This gives confidence to everyone. Give a few of your own responses to set a respectful and helpful tone, and encourage others in the class to respond. Take note of both the content and the skills demonstrated by the writer.

Examples of Encouraging Responses

- I'm impressed with your use of dialogue. It's hard to write in different voices so that the different speakers sound like individuals. You do a good job of that.
- Did everyone notice how she used colors in her descriptions, so you really feel like you're in the room with her?
- A lot of times, kids your age have conflicts with their parents. This sounds like it was really hard for you and your dad.
- Could you read the description of the car one more time? You used a lot of great details in that passage.
- You might feel responsible for your friend's suicide, but it's not your fault. If something like this happens to anyone in this class, be sure to talk to an adult about it.
- There might be other people in the class who have been through something like that but didn't know how to write about it. Thank you.
- We might need to know a little more about what happened before the fight. Does anyone have any specific questions about that?
- Was anyone confused by the mixture of Spanish and English, or were you able to figure out what everyone was saying?
- I know how hard it is to write about that. Nice job.

Again, leave time for bringing the session to a close, acknowledging that this kind of writing takes a different kind of effort than much of what students do in school. Thank the students for their good work.

Responding to Second Drafts

As you read second drafts, you will have much more to work with. Often, by now, the writing has begun to take shape and the students have put a lot of thought into what they are trying to say. Remember that the more effort your students put into their writing, the more vulnerable they may feel about your response to it. When anyone writes about something close to the heart, criticism of the writing may be felt as criticism of the person. For that reason, be careful about correcting or editing in the traditional sense.

Make it clear that you want to understand what the writer has to say. If something interferes with that understanding, ask for clarity with a question mark penciled in above an indecipherable word or a suggestion that it would be easier to understand the dialogue if each speaker's voice were in a separate paragraph.

This kind of gentle care with student writing takes more time than the cryptic comments or editing marks most teachers must struggle to find time to make, but it is important as a way of establishing trust. Once your students know that you care about what they are writing, you can use shorthand notations for some of the mechanical details. You can teach a few symbols for the most common notations and have a poster or handout or overhead transparency with those notations on it so that students can refer to it as they read your comments. Mixing positive and negative notations encourages students to read all of them.

At this stage — beyond the freewriting, rough-draft stage, but not yet ready for fine-tuning or precise editing — you are still coaxing the writing out. Again, use a highlighter to call attention to anything you like, for any reason. It's an easy way to offer encouragement and to subtly change student expectations about your response to their writing. Students who are used to thinking that the more marks someone has made on their paper, the worse it is, have to rethink (or refeel) their response to your hard work on behalf of their writing.

Figure 5–4

	Notations for Teacher Response
☆	Great image!
?	I don't understand this. Could you explain it in more detail?
¶	Start a new paragraph here.
!	I know what you mean.
s p	Spelling mistake. Use a dictionary or spell-checker.
W	I'm not sure this is the word you want. Talk to me about this.
P	A punctuation problem is causing confusion.
☺	This makes me smile.
☹	This made me cry.
V	Your verb tenses don't agree. Let me know if you need help fixing this.

For Poetry:

/	Try breaking your line here.
//	Try starting a new stanza here (skip a line).
[ ]	Maybe you don't need the words inside the brackets.

Some students may have run out of time halfway through something they are working on, and you can just write something like, "I can't wait to read the rest of this. Keep going!" Others may have written a couple of lines of a poem, half a page of a story, or a few exchanges of dialogue in a script and think they are finished. In such cases, ask a few specific questions to let them know you think there is more to the story.

Peer response is also effective at this point and can be helpful in the face of limitations on a teacher's time. In pairs or small groups, students can share their writing with one another, and you can instruct them to ask specific questions about anything that is either unclear ("I don't get it.") or intriguing ("Tell me more."). Then the writers can go back to work and try to respond to those questions.

6
Shaping, Polishing, and Publishing

As you embark on the final stage of a writing project, you will need considerable flexibility in how you spend your classroom time, particularly for the longer writing activities. Some students will be struggling to finish a first draft while others will be ready to work on polishing a final draft. Writing will vary in length, and the authors' definitions of finished work are likely to fall into a wide range. You may want to suggest that the students have a book to read, so that if they finish before the rest of the class they can read quietly without distracting those who are still writing.

Encourage and assist your students in doing their own editing wherever possible, but consider the possibility of typing and editing their work for them once or twice so that they can see what their writing looks like in an edited and typed form. If you can see into a rough version of a story or a poem and pull out the gem of writing within it, you will help your students see the value in their own writing and they will be more motivated to learn how to polish and edit on their own.

The final stages of writing will be different for each genre, but I offer some general guidelines in the following sections.

Formal or Informal Voice
This is a good time to raise the question of the degree of formality students are aiming for in their writing. For some straight narrative writing, a highly

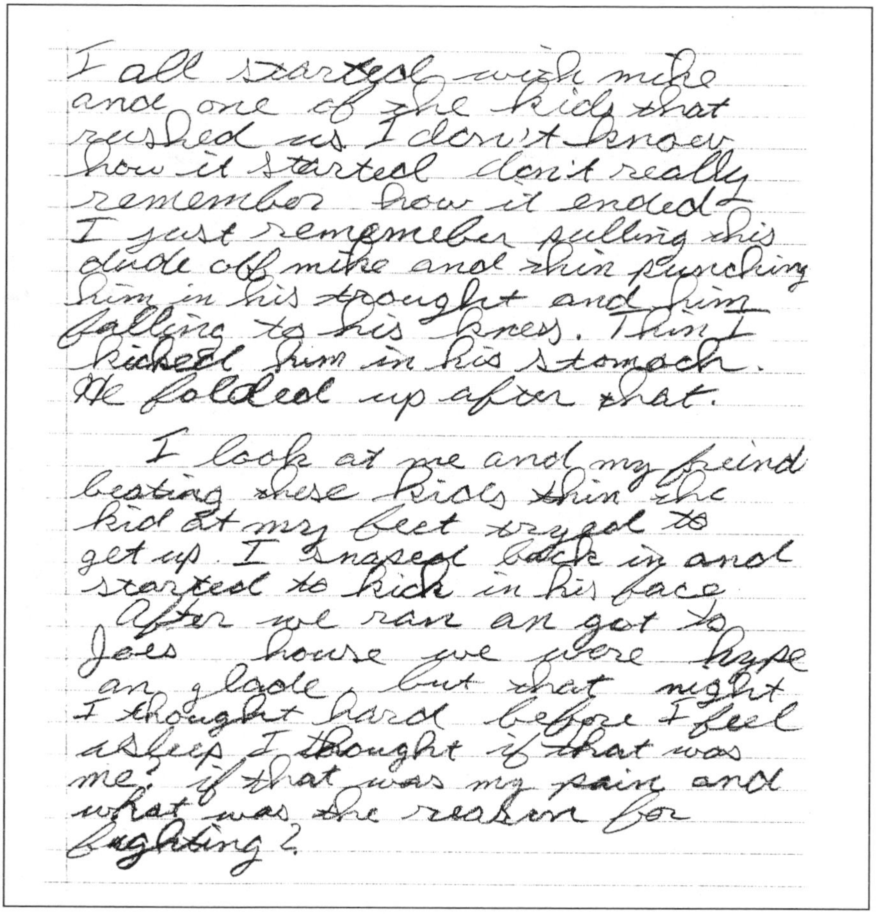
I all started with mike
and one of the kids that
rushed us I don't know
how it started don't really
remember how it ended
I just remember pulling this
dude off mike and thin punching
him in his trought and him
falling to his knees. Thin I
kicked him in his stomach.
He folded up after that.

I look at me and my feind
beating these kids thin the
kid at my feet tryed to
get up. I snaped back in and
started to kick in his face
After we ran an got to
Joes house we were hype
an glade, but that night
I thought hard before I feel
asleep I thought if that was
me, if that was my pain and
what was the reason for
fighting?

Figure 6–1 Final draft of "Pain" (p. 84), handed in for typing.

formal voice is the most effective; students should know how to write in formal English. But if they are writing in the voice of a character who uses slang words or an informal tone, they should know how to make the writing sound like that person is talking.

Some students want their whole story to be in an informal voice ("That's how I talk!" or "I want it to sound like my grandma!"). Others want their writing to be more formal but may not be sure of how to achieve that. Discuss this in class, giving them copies of writing in different styles and asking them what the voice lets them know about the speaker and why or how they know that. For examples of intentional use of informal voice see

"Eat Dirt" by Constance García-Barrio (p. 106), and my poem "White Walls" (p. 69).

If students choose to use an informal style, discuss the importance of consistency and clarity. If they want to write in a formal style but are not skilled at it, offer to help them. In either case, say things like, "In this line, do you want to use *has* or *have*?" or, "Would this character say *mine* or *mines*?"

Point out that sometimes the narration may be more formal than the dialogue. If a student writes, "My father say he don't care what I do, long as I stay out of jail," show how, in formal English, that would be written, "My father says he doesn't care what I do, as long as I stay out of jail," and ask which style the student wants to use. In a direct quote, the informal style often gives a better sense of the speaker's voice: "He don't care what you do, long as you stay out of jail," my mother told me.

It's important to treat this as a stylistic issue, rather than as an issue of right and wrong, or "good English" and "bad English." Students already know how to change from one kind of speech to another: what is appropriate among friends at a party is different from what is expected in a job interview. Encourage them to be aware of how authors change styles in written language.

Words You Can't Use in School

In this final stage of polishing the writing, the use of "appropriate language" often arises. I put that phrase in quotes because it is such a loaded expression, with such didactic overtones, that I don't want to use it without taking a good look at what it actually means and how it has come to be used. Lots of words you can't use in school are perfectly appropriate in other situations.

For example, Constance García-Barrio, in the original version of "Eat Dirt" (p. 106), used the word *ass*, where the version that appears in this book uses *pockets*. The original is completely appropriate to what the author intends, giving the speaker a delightfully audacious voice. Still, knowing that teachers would be giving this writing to students, and students reporting to parents, and some parents complaining to principals, I felt I had to ask the author if I could change that one word for use in this book. We talked at some length about alternatives: *pockets* throws off the rhythm; *shoes* isn't right; really, this character would say *ass*. It is with considerable regret that we decided on *pockets* as the "appropriate language" in this instance.

Your students may offer similar arguments: "But that was what caused the fight! I can't write the story without using that word!" If that happens, treat it as a problem to be solved, and ask the class to help: "Can anyone think of a way to get the essence of this scene without using that word?" If "bad" words are essential to the story and you cannot allow your students to use them, I suggest using the first letter followed by dashes, or symbolic characters: %#*(.

Revision Checklist

As students work on the final copy of their writing, ask them to pay attention to these things:

- Spelling: Use a dictionary, ask for help, or, if using a computer, run a spell-check program.
- Punctuation: Read the piece out loud and see if the punctuation tells you when to pause, when to stop, and when each person starts and stops speaking.
- Structure: In prose, are all the sentences in each paragraph related? In poetry, have you made line breaks and stanza breaks for a reason?
- Clarity: Will the reader know what you mean?
- Music: Do you like the way the language sounds?

Reading Finished Work Out Loud

When most of the students have finished their writing, offer them an opportunity to share it with their classmates. If students are reluctant to read, I say, "If your story is too personal, and you don't want to read it for that reason, I understand that, and we'll all respect your privacy. But if you don't want to read because you don't have confidence in your story, that's not a good reason. Other people will appreciate your writing just as you appreciate theirs." Usually, the reading snowballs: one brave person reads and receives an appreciative response, then one or two more dare to read, and eventually most of the class will have read. If there is not enough time for everyone to read, assure the students that you will finish the next day.

Be prepared for the emotional impact of this reading. Some students have written about very raw and recent events, others about things that happened some years ago but are still unresolved. One girl's story about her brother's suicide struck me as slightly overdramatic the first time I read it. I was about to suggest that she tone it down a little, but when I asked her how long ago this had happened, she replied, "A week and two days." I was astounded that she could write about it at all. Don't rush through the reading if stories or poems invite responsive discussion, but try not to get bogged down on any one story either.

Be sure to acknowledge the courage of the writers and the maturity of the listeners. If they have, in fact, shared stories or poems of things they have been holding inside themselves, and if they have received one another's words with respect, be aware that this in itself is a major accomplishment for many young people. There is still work to be done, if the stories are to be published, but the mechanics of writing have been transformed from a list of arbitrary rules into a set of details to be learned and applied to a meaningful task.

This is a good time to take one more long, deep breath and let it out, in gratitude for the beauty and intelligence of each human being and for our ability to recognize that in one another.

Final Editing and Publication

Never require publication of any kind of personal writing. Some students will gain a great deal from the experience of writing, but will not want anyone else to read what they have written. These writers should still be encouraged to make a final, clean copy of their work, and if a grade is involved, you will need to see what they have done. It may not be perfect, but it should be their best work.

For students who wish to publish their work, publication can be an incentive to give extra attention to the final editing and polishing stages of writing. If you have some students who have good editing skills, peer editing can be helpful at this stage. Encourage your students to ask one another for help as they prepare their writing for publication.

Publication simply means "to make public." This can happen in any number of ways:

- Put each paper up on a bulletin board for others to read.
- Compile a collection of stories or poems and make multiple copies.
- Create a short skit or play and perform it.
- Let one class exchange its stories or poems with another class.

If you decide to create an anthology of student work, there are two possibilities: an anthology in which everyone's work is included or one for which an editor or an editorial committee selects the best work. In my experience, an inclusive anthology is usually more worthwhile, though it may be possible to do both.

In one school, I do a one-week residency in an eighth-grade classroom each November, and every year we publish an anthology that includes one poem by each student. Now there are nine anthologies, and they have become historical documents as well as resources for teaching poetry. Each year, the eighth graders spend time looking through past anthologies, finding poems by older siblings, cousins, and friends. Some of the former student-poets have gone on to college, some are in prison, and a few have died, but in these treasured collections, we have a record of something — an image, a memory, a little joke, a serious thought — from each of them.

Tap the talents of the class for artwork and cover design and, in the case of older students, for typing and layout. This is a big project that will require considerable leadership and supervision.

If possible, make enough copies so that each student can have two copies and one copy can be placed in the school and public libraries. You may want to give copies to school board members and other teachers. Some schools include the cost of this as a line item in the budget; others ask for support from local businesses; others sell some copies at a high enough price to pay for the students' free copies.

PREPARING THE MANUSCRIPT

If you are typing and editing the anthology yourself, type the poems and stories as you think the students want them to appear. Before collecting the stories to type, tell the students that you will fix any spelling mistakes they missed, and ask them to write "informal" or "formal" on their papers to indicate whether or not they want you to correct grammar irregularities.

Always return a copy of the typed and edited work to the author for final proofreading. Students are meticulous editors at this stage, catching things you may have missed and making final, often subtle, adjustments to their writing.

However you approach questions of publication, the essential thing is that the writers remain involved in their own writing and view editing and publication as the final step in making their valuable stories available to others. Continue saying things like, "This is so interesting (or beautiful, or funny, or touching). I want to be sure your reader understands exactly what you mean."

PUBLISHING AN ANTHOLOGY

There are several ways to publish an anthology of student writing. Get information several months in advance so you know exactly what you will need to do and what the cost and deadline will be.

A collection of everyone's writing can be typed up, photocopied in-house, and distributed among one or two classes or to all the students in one grade. Sometimes students in one grade can create a book for students in a younger grade.

You can also have your book professionally printed. The value in this is that young writers see such a book as being real, and that helps them feel connected to other things they read.

Some students may want to submit their stories and poems to contests or to state or national publications. Give them as much information as they need so that they can make realistic decisions. Publication in a school literary magazine will carry honor and, with support from you, should be within range of all students. Publication in a state or national publication is less likely, but it may be more exciting when it happens. Alert students to the fact that they should never pay to be published and they should be suspicious of any publication that tries to sell the writers an expensive copy of the book in which their writing appears.

CELEBRATE!

If you have created an anthology, plan an event for the release date. This may be something as simple as just allowing class time to read the books. Susan Harroff, the eighth-grade teacher in whose classroom I teach each year, describes her class on the day the books are distributed: "I allow each class twenty minutes to read silently and then to stand and read aloud to the class any poem that they particularly like — their own or that of another student. Students always do so with great enthusiasm, and several classes have stayed into the passing period, not wanting to break into their reading until I insist that they leave. Many of the students who have read with great seriousness, clarity, and expression are those who have shown little motivation in other academic endeavors."

If you wish to have a more formal book release event, invite parents and school board members to your class and have students go to the front of the room and read their poems and stories or present their scripts. Serve refreshments and allow time for students to sign one another's books.

If school board members can't come to your class, ask if they would like to invite some of the students to one of their meetings to present copies of the book and read one or two selections from it.

Finally, when all the work is finished, look back with pride on a big accomplishment. Where did you begin, and where have you traveled together? What surprises did you meet along the way? Give your students an opportunity to acknowledge what they have done and talk to one another about the content of their writing. This genuine conversation about things that really matter to them is something they will remember for a long time.

7
Poetry

The Portrait

My mother never forgave my father
for killing himself,
especially at such an awkward time
and in a public park,
that spring
when I was waiting to be born.
She locked his name
in her deepest cabinet
and would not let him out,
though I could hear him thumping.
When I came down from the attic
with the pastel portrait in my hand
of a long-lipped stranger
with a brave moustache
and deep brown level eyes,
she ripped it into shreds
without a single word
and slapped me hard.
In my sixty-fourth year
I can feel my cheek
still burning.

—Stanley Kunitz

When children hear or read this poem, it gives them access to their own deepest cabinets, their own portraits of courage, their own still-burning cheeks. It shows them that there are ways to speak of the difficult things in life, those things they have been taught not to talk about.

Poetry is a special universe where people meet and understand each other through images and the music of language. Of all the genres, it is the one that reluctant writers are often most willing to try. Lots of teenagers and preteens have a poetry notebook hidden away in a closet at home, full of poems they have memorized, copied down, or composed in the middle of the night. If you allow or invite them to do so, they will bring these poems into the classroom, and if you have created a safe atmosphere, they will eagerly share them with you and their classmates.

Poetry often appeals to students who aren't good at other kinds of writing. They can see things in a nonlinear way, and they can enjoy playing with words on the page and discovering what happens when they put sounds and images together. Or maybe they just see that poetry can be short. They can write a poem in one class period and feel pretty good about it. The stages of revision and polishing are not too daunting, because the text is a manageable length.

In writing about emotional topics, the images of poetry offer a way into the emotion. Then, finding the form a poem takes can give young writers control over those emotions.

In this chapter, I offer specific activities to help you teach your students to write poems. (For further resources, see Appendix A.) As you try these activities, read lots of poetry with your students. Send them to the library with instructions to "Call 811" (the Dewey decimal system number for American poetry) and find a poem that matters to them. Reading good poetry carries the reader into the place where poetry happens. Let your students experience poetry in that way first, simply welcoming the gifts it offers; later, when they have come to love poetry, you can help them learn to read more analytically.

In most of the activities, I have suggested a way of writing a collaborative poem with the entire class before asking students to write individual poems. Collaborative poems are especially helpful in a classroom where students lack confidence. They take the pressure off individual students, while still allowing them to see themselves as poets. I like to do several collaborations early on in my work with a class and come back to them as warm-ups later on. In some collaborations, you will have more suggestions than you can fit into the group poem; if that happens, tell the students to write down those ideas and use them in poems of their own.

One-Liners

If your students are intimidated by the very idea of writing a poem, one-liners are a good way to break the ice. All they have to think of is one line.

For one-liner collaborations, give the first few words of a line, and invite each person in the class to complete the line in his or her own words. Here are a few starter ideas for one-liners. You or your students may think of others.

- I want to stay alive . . . (or I want to live to see . . .)
- I used to be/I am now/I am becoming . . . (three separate but related poems or one three-stanza poem)
- I am not afraid of . . .
- I am afraid of . . .
- Most people don't know . . .
- Believe me . . .
- I remember . . .
- I hope . . .
- It isn't fair . . .
- I wish I'd known . . .

The following poem, "Staying Alive," was spoken and written with a group of teenage boys who had a hard time believing that they would live to be adults. Speaking a vision of the future took considerable courage.

Staying Alive

I want to live to see different parts of the world, maybe Japan.
I want to see if I will have a family.
I want to see my daughter grow up and get married.
I want to live so I can see what my child will be like: me or her mother.
I want to stay alive so I can get married and have a kid of my own.
I want to stay alive because I have much more things to see and do.
I want to see my son or daughter ride the bus to the first day of school.
I want to see what I may become: governor, astronaut, or a great general.
I want to raise a family and see how the world is 40 years from now.
I want to stay alive to see my kids become something special in life.
I want to stay alive to see if I will ever become rich and have a wife.
I want to stay alive because I want to have a wife and kids.
I want to see the way my people change their lives and live differently in
   the future.

SPEAKING AND WRITING A ONE-LINER GROUP POEM

Read "Staying Alive" or "I Am Not Afraid" (p. 54 or p. 63). Ask students which lines they remember. If they remember the most vivid, specific lines, point out that specific details make writing more memorable.

After going over the rules for safety (no teasing), have each person speak a line that he or she has created, beginning with the words of the starter. To keep the poem moving, let anyone pass on the first round, and then come back to those who passed after others have contributed. After everyone has contributed or passed more than once, ask each person to write down his or her line so you or a volunteer from the class can type the entire poem.

Return a copy of the whole poem to each contributor, and ask someone to read it to the class, or have each person read one line, not necessarily his or her own.

INDIVIDUAL POEMS FROM ONE-LINERS

Ask the students to elaborate on their own one-liners to create individual poems. Ask them to create a specific image, using details of time and place, maybe using a color or naming a sound or a smell. Suggest that they write the poem in the present tense, as if the imagined image is actually happening. For example, the following poem was developed from "I want to see if I will have a family."

> My wife comes into the kitchen carrying our son Kyler
> and he reaches out his arms to me. I can smell
> his dirty diaper. When he smiles, I can't help
> smiling back. He reaches up and pulls
> on the gold chain around my neck.

Then ask each student to choose one line, not his or her own, and write a poem in response, creating a more specific vision of what the line would mean. The following example was created from "I want to see my son or daughter ride the bus to the first day of school."

> You deserve to walk to the school bus
> with your daughter Melanie, holding her hand,
> telling her how you got to drink chocolate milk
> and play with giant Lego blocks
> on your first day of school.

Ask each person to make two copies of his or her poem, giving one to the person whose line was used, and keeping one copy.

Writing About an Object

An indirect approach is often safer than writing directly about private feelings. As students imagine what an inanimate object or an animal might be feeling, they can touch on precarious things in their own lives without revealing more than they want to. It also gives them a way to practice compassion; it might be hard to admit that they feel sorry for the kid everyone is picking on, but they can express compassion, and perhaps empathy, by writing about the poor basketball that gets thrown and bounced around all day long.

"Tree" (p. 63) was written by a group of students on a stormy night, imagining together how a tree might feel. Some students thought the tree would be terrified, while others thought it would be calm and strong. I suspected that the images the different students were offering about the tree might reflect their own internal struggles, and I helped them shape the poem so that all their different ideas could be included and the poem could end on a hopeful note.

Begin this activity by reading "Tree" to the class or by passing out copies or putting it on an overhead and reading it together. Then discuss: If the tree is like a person, what would the person be feeling? How does that change from the beginning of the poem to the end? The poem is in free verse, but there is a pattern to it. Can you see the symmetry in the number of lines in each stanza? (First verse balanced with the last verse, second balanced with second to last.) How is that like the structure of a tree? Notice, too, how the poem looks "tall" on the page.

Next, ask for ideas of something to write about: the sky, a car, an alley, a highway, a potato, a hammer, a wolf, a cat, a basketball. Choose one idea, reminding the students to hold onto other ideas for individual poems. Ask for suggestions about what the object or animal might experience and how it might feel. Write down all the suggestions; if different ideas contradict each other, see if your students can figure out a way to work with the contradictions.

Ask questions to generate more specific images. If someone says the tree hears a saw, ask: What kind of saw? How far away is it? Is the sound constant or on and off? If someone says the other trees are jealous, ask why.

Ask if anyone sees a pattern. Which images go together? What order should we put them in? Shape the poem according to the pattern.

Type up the poem and return a copy to each collaborator. Ask someone to read it aloud, and take suggestions for revision.

Next, have students write individual poems about—or in the voice of—an object or an animal. Bring in a large basket of natural objects (rocks, feathers, bones, nests, shells, cicada skins, etc.) or photographs of animals in their natural settings, and let each student choose one to write about. Often writers will describe their own feelings in terms of the objects or animals they select, but there is no pressure to do so. Layna's poem expresses what a lot of middle school students feel about navigating the crowded hallways in their day-to-day lives:

The Wolf
I am like a young wolf that runs freely through the woods.
When I'm in trouble, I like to test my strength.
I travel close to my pack every day
because I know if I go astray, instead of
hunter, I will become the prey.

These can be whole poems, but they can also help students find images in more complex poems. See "Maybe . . ." (p. 65) for an example of how a student integrates an image of a volleyball into a more complex poem.

Using Images to Define Emotions
It's hard for many students to talk about their feelings. To help them get started, you can use my Image Worksheet (p. 128) and Conversation with a Feeling Worksheet (p. 129) to offer them ways to use specific imagery to define emotions.

Tim Seibles' poem "Kerosene" (p. 66) and Ingrid Wendt's "Middle Sister Poem" (p. 65) offer a good introduction to these lessons. Read the poems with your students and invite them to discuss the imagery in the poems, noting particularly how the authors use images to describe feelings.

Then, with your students, make a list of different emotions: fear, joy, sadness, jealousy, anger, loneliness, confusion, and so on. Make a list of images, encouraging students to be specific. Some ideas to get you started: a crescent moon, a cracked sidewalk, a quarter stuck in a parking meter, a three-legged dog, five eggs in a robin's nest, a blue car driving slowly down the street at midnight.

Ask if someone can find one emotion and one image that are nothing like each other. For example: "Anger is nothing like a three-legged dog." Challenge the class to find a way in which the emotion and the image can be compared. Can anyone see how anger *is* like a three-legged dog? Not how or why a three-legged dog might *be* angry, but how it might *represent* anger. If someone suggests, "You know how, when you're mad, you just look for

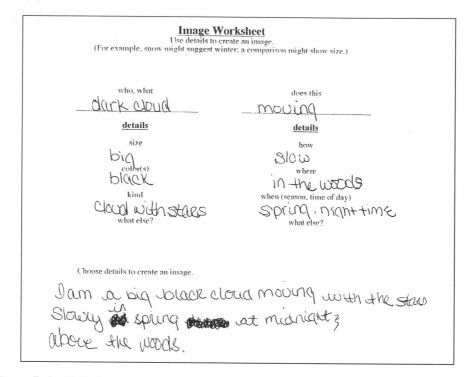

Figure 7–1   Nella's poem, created using the Image worksheet. The worksheet encourages students to expand their images.

things that will make you even more mad, like a dog smelling for meat?" that might be refined into a poem. Use the Image worksheet as an overhead to help develop an image such as the following:

> Anger is like a three-legged dog
> limping along a dark street
> nosing into every garbage can
> growling when anyone gets too close.

Ask the class to make a decision about whether you need the word *like* in the first line.

Next, ask each student to write an individual poem that describes an emotion by using an image. They can use the lists you have generated together or make up images of their own. Give each student a copy of the Image Worksheet, telling them it's a tool, not a formula. They should use it to generate ideas and then pick and choose among those ideas to get the image they

Image Worksheet
Use details to create an image.
(For example, snow might suggest winter; a comparison might show size.)

who, what

brain

details

size *big*

color(s) *blue*

kind *rigid*

what else?

does this

exploding

details

how *slowly*

where *mouth*

when (season, time of day) *midnight*

what else? *sleeping*

Choose details to create an image.

My blue brain is exploding slowly out of my mouth while I'm sleeping at midnight.

Translation: For doing wrong in the day I'm getting punished when I least expect it, when I'm sleep.

(Save from doing bad.)

Figure 7–2 *"Special K" discovers something about herself through an image.*

like. For example, if someone writes, "Fear is like a cat," the worksheet asks what kind and color of cat it is, what the cat is doing, and so on. The student will get lots of ideas, which can then be boiled down to something like: "Fear is a fat orange cat, arching its back, hissing at the moon."

CONVERSATION WITH A FEELING
This is a possible follow-up to the last poem. If you haven't done the previous lesson, spend some time teaching what an image is and how to make it spe-

Talking to my _Angerness_ (name a feeling)

When (write something that happened)

when my little brother told
my boyfreind I collect
dolls

My _angerness_ (name of feeling, same as in title) **was like**

a getto ninja doll ready
to go to war

I spoke to my _Angerness_ (name of feeling) **and said**

we will calm down
after the war

And it answered

Stop youill get in trouble

I answered back

so who cares

Figure 7–3   Two students converse with different emotions (see Figure 7–4).

cific. Read "Middle Sister Poem" (p. 65) and "Maybe . . ." (p. 65) and ask the students to think of something specific that has happened to them and try to describe how they felt about it by using an image.

Put the Conversation with a Feeling worksheet on an overhead and do an example together. Then pass out copies of the worksheet and ask students to fill in an emotion in the blank space and then use the form to help them write a poem about that emotion. Tell them to use the form in any way it is useful. They can repeat lines they like or leave out lines they don't like. The conversation can go on longer if they wish. They can leave the form and go off in their own direction at any point. They don't have to fill in every line.

Figure 7–4 Two students converse with different emotions (see Figure 7–3).

Circulate among the students as they are writing, encouraging them to relax into their writing and to elaborate on their images and ideas. For those students who finish quickly, ask them to get together with someone who wrote about a different emotion and see if they can write a conversation between two emotions: "Sadness Speaks to Joy" or "Jealousy Speaks to Fear."

Writing in a Given Form: Tritina

This is a more challenging form of poetry. It often allows students to attempt a subject that they want to write about and don't know how to approach.

Begin by handing out copies of "The Bird" (p. 69) and "Day of Sadness" (p. 64), or put the poems on an overhead and read them with your students. Read the examples twice. On the first reading, don't pay any attention to the form; just read for meaning. On the second reading, note how the form works.

Next, use a Tritina worksheet (p. 130) to show students how the form works, with three end words in each of three stanzas repeating in a particular order and then used again in a final line.

Suggest that students think of a particular incident or place they want to describe or a person they want to address. On a piece of blank paper, have them write one word that they might want to use in their poem. Then give them two or three minutes to free-associate from that one word, writing as many words as they can all over their paper. If they haven't done this before, demonstrate on the blackboard or overhead: write the word *house* and let everyone call out the first word that comes to mind. Write their words as fast as you can: blue, family, street, porch, kitchen, window. When you have five or six words, branch off from each of them with whatever words come to mind. For example: blue—dress, mother, eyes, car, sky, night; family—sister, music, loud, Dad, shout, cuss, bottle.

Ask them to circle any three words on their free-association paper and try to use those three words as their end words. If they get stuck, they can go back to the paper to see if other words will work better. Give students copies of the Tritina worksheet to work with as they write.

Follow-up For Ambitious Students: Sestina

If your students are interested, a similar, but more complex form is the sestina. Six end words repeat in a particular order in six stanzas, followed by a three-line stanza that uses all six end words, two in each line.

The order of the end words is abcdef, faebdc, cfdabe, ecbfad, deacfb, bdfeca (each letter stands for a word). The traditional order of the end words in the three lines of the envoy is be, dc, fa. The first of the two words is somewhere within the line and the second word ends the line. See my poems "White Walls" (p. 69) and "I Look Around and Wonder" (p. 71) for examples of the sestina form.

This is just a beginning, of course. I hope it will entice you to give poetry a central place in your classroom all year round, not just during a once-a-year poetry unit. Poetry will bring you and your students closer to each other and to the other poets whose work you read. Reading poetry helps students write it, and writing poetry helps them read it.

Poetry Examples: Student Writing

Sometimes students who seem to pose a threat to others are the ones who are most scared themselves. And it is scary for young people to know that they frighten other people. A group of girls sorted through those feelings in this group poem:

I Am Not Afraid

I am not afraid of police.
I am not afraid of jail.
I am not afraid of the judge.
I am not afraid of my parents.
I am not afraid of ghosts.
I am not afraid of the dark.
I am not afraid of Mike.
I am not afraid of dogs, cats, or snakes.
I am not afraid of Jesus, or God.
I am not afraid of horses.
You don't need to be afraid of me.
I'm not going to beat you up.
I'm a nice person.
I'm me.
I'm not afraid of anyone.
You don't need to be afraid of me.

Tree

The tree stands tall and terrified
branches cracking in the wind.
Its trunk sways
but does not break.

Afraid of every sound,
it stands there listening.
Termites inside it,
birds in its branches,
leaves blowing off,

chainsaws in the distance.

It's jealous of the evergreens,
laughing at it in the winter
when it is naked
and they are not.

But in the spring
when it gets its coat back,
the evergreens look hot,
standing there wishing for rain.
They get all sticky,
and they never get to change their clothes.

The tree stands tall and cool.
Its roots push and stretch
cradled by the soil.
Absorbing cool moisture,
the roots hold the tree
however tall it grows.

Now birds land
and peck out the tree's bugs.
The tree stretches wide and strong.
Squirrels play on its branches.

— Group poem

"Day of Sadness" is a tritina written by an eighth grader who had witnessed the murder of her mother. Mindy had not told her teacher or her classmates about this, and it was a big decision for her to write her poem and read it out loud.

Day of Sadness

I still remember that day of sadness.
I cried and cried and just couldn't stop crying.
The sounding of the gun.

I miss her comforting touch, all I can do is cry.
I remember the sounding of the gun.
Then all the sadness began.

The gun
will cause all my sadness.
Forever I will cry.

If it weren't for the gun, I wouldn't have to be sad
and I wouldn't have to cry.

—Mindy

Note: Mindy uses repeating words, but she changes *sadness* to *sad*, and
crying to *cry*. Also, in stanza 2, the word *sadness* comes before the end of the
line. It was more important to Mindy to say what she wanted to say about this
significant, terrible memory than it was to follow the form exactly. Most
poets who work in given forms allow themselves this kind of freedom.

Maybe . . .

As I listen to my parents argue,
sitting on the couch wondering
what's going to happen,
I feel like a volleyball,
being spiked, and falling to the ground.

As they fight, I ask myself, why me?
What did I do to deserve this?
Then I answer myself,
Maybe I do deserve this, maybe I caused this.

As I sit and wait, listening
to what my parents are saying
I keep thinking
       Maybe I caused this,
       Maybe I deserve this,
Maybe I don't

—Nikki

Adult Writing

Middle Sister Poem

Real as the ridge
line children draw sharp on the edge
of mountains, there's a point

friendship sometimes will reach,
thin as a footstep between
east and west, where one of you

won't go on and the wind
to the other says *Don't look*
back or you're gone.

Up ahead, the peak
you can climb
alone. And then?

—*Ingrid Wendt*

Ingrid Wendt is the author of two books of poetry and a book about teaching poetry, as well as the editor of several anthologies. She lives in Eugene, Oregon. She writes this about "Middle Sister Poem":

Most people who read "Middle Sister Poem" don't know the title is also the name of a mountain, between Bend and Eugene, Oregon, in the Cascade range. There are three mountains, in fact: North Sister, Middle Sister, and South Sister: cone-shaped and close together, all in a row, joined near their tops by high rock walls.

When I wrote this poem, I'd been haunted by memories of the day I'd hiked up the Middle Sister, several years before, with a good friend, and of the way our friendship later seemed to fall away. Was it because she got scared, up near the top (where the ridge line is), and I chose not to sit and wait, with her, for the rest of our group to finish the climb and return? Part of me knew I could—and maybe should—have stayed with her, to keep her company; but I had a life, too, I thought, and reaching the top was important to me. And so I went on, leaving her (temporarily) behind.

Maybe it's like that with all friendships that fail: there really is a moment—not necessarily on a mountain—when people face challenges together, when choices must be made. When, in order to be truly themselves, friends choose different paths. They aren't sure they've done the right things. There may be no one person to blame. But there's no going back to the way things were.

Poem first published in *Singing the Mozart Requiem*, Breitenbush Books, Inc., 1987.

Kerosene

* after the L.A. riot, April 1992
In my country   the weather
it's not too good   At every bus stop anger

holds her umbrella folded her
face buckled tight as a boot   Along the avenues
beneath parked cars spent
cartridges glimmer   A man's head crushed
by nightsticks   smoke still
slides from his mouth   Let out wearing

uniforms   hyenas rove in packs
unmuzzled and brothers strain inside
their brown skins   like something wounded
thrown into a lake   Slowly
like blood filling
cracks in the street slowly the
President   arrived   his mouth
slit into his face   Like candles seen
through thick curtains   sometimes
at night   the dark citizens
occur to him

like fishing lamps along
the black shore of a lake   like moths
soaked in kerosene   and lit

—Tim Seibles

*George Bush Sr. was in office at this time.

Tim Seibles is the author of five collections of poetry, most recently *Hammerlock*. He teaches at Old Dominion University in Norfolk, Virginia. He writes this about "Kerosene":

I chose to use various breaks in the lines of this poem rather than standard punctuation because I wanted the poem to have the feel and movement of someone thinking aloud. All of our thinking is marked by hesitations as we consider and re-consider what it is we're trying to clarify. In this poem I'm trying to mesh a smoldering rage with a meditative cool in an effort to write a poem that is both intellectually clear and emotionally honest. I want the *caesuras* to mark the pauses caused by an attempt to balance these two aspects of thinking.

"Kerosene" first appeared in the chapbook *Kerosene*, published by Ampersand Press. It is included in Seibles' full-length collection *Hammerlock*, published by Cleveland State University (1999).

Watermelon Hill

Close the door and never look back.
This is finished for you now.
—Sister Marie Dolores

After she got herself in trouble, they sent her
away to Watermelon Hill, which was not really
its name, but what the boys yelled to the swollen girls
who were to come due at that home for unwed mothers.
A crucifix glared from the roof.
Laurel Taylor was not her real name.
What was real was absolved by Mother
Superior with a flap of her cloak.
Under the Immaculate Heart of Mary
was posted a litany of daily chores.
Miles of buffed linoleum, bars on the windows,
Doctor Crutchfield on Wednesdays, jelly jars
filled with vitamins. The tables were set for forty
or so, depending on who was in labor.
The tuna casseroles smelled like bleach.
Girls back from the hospital sat on donut pillows.
Days passed and the moon sickened.

Laurel Taylor, on her horrible cot with the stars
moving inside her, tried to pray.
It was best to give up your baby, not see or hold it.
It was best to place your baby, make a plan for it.

Laurel Taylor tried to pray in the chapel,
her cardigan sweater open like a gate.
She fought to be good, to give her blood to some
nice family, to cleanse a child from her name.
Laurel Taylor tried to keep the monsters away
but under some god's baleful eye, they rose
in a spine-cramping pain that was only the start
of the tearing off.

She lost her son in that war. Wading in water,
being able to see her feet again, she knew there would be
no anointing, no Extreme Unction.
After signing the surrender, she knew
the penance is fault and the loss is eternal.
—Linda Back McKay

Linda Back McKay has written four books of poetry and nonfiction including the book *Shadow Mothers: Stories of Adoption and Reunion.* A play based on this poem portrays women who met as teenage "unwed mothers" as they reunite years later and discuss their lives.

Linda writes this about her poem:

The experience of writing *Shadow Mothers* brought down an avalanche of emotion from the past that resulted in a series of poems, including "Watermelon Hill." The artistic director of the Great American History Theatre heard me on Minnesota Public Radio reading the poem. He called me, we met, and that is how the idea for the play, *Watermelon Hill,* came to be.

The Bird

Grandma keeps forgetting that my grandpa died.
She asks us where he is, why he's been gone
so long. And if we say, *Remember*?

He had a heart attack, she tries to remember
but she can't. We have to tell her that he died.
That makes her mad. So now we say he's gone

to someplace nice. She's glad he hasn't gone
to war again. It wasn't always like this. I remember
once when I was little, we found a bird that died.

What's 'died'? I asked. She said, *the bird is gone, but we remember.*

—Helen Frost

I wrote this tritina in the voice of a fictional child, about eleven years old. "White Walls" and "I Look Around and Wonder" are sestinas in the voices of fictional teenagers.

"White Walls" is in the voice of Carmen, a fifteen-year old girl who has been locked up for driving under the influence of alcohol.

White Walls

Carmen

I wasn't drunk. Just one beer a couple hours
before. Never woulda got stopped
if I was an adult. Or if I was white.
That half-smoked blunt they found under the back
seat—how would I know it was there?
Coulda been there since Grandmama

bought the car, five months ago. Grandmama
wouldn't think to look for that! Visiting hours
is over, and she didn't show up. Only one there
all week was my probation officer. She stopped
by for ten minutes, said she was *so unhappy* to see me back
in here, got out a clean white

note pad and asked me for an explanation. *No little white
lies,* she said. I asked her to call Grandmama
and tell her I'm sorry, see if I can go back
there when I get outta here. That was hours
ago, and I haven't heard from either of 'em. Can't stop
thinkin about what's gonna happen. If I can't go back there . . .

I don't know. Could be a long ways, anyhow, from here to there.
I talked to one girl today, a white
girl that's been here thirteen weeks. She stopped
thinkin about home, she said. *Forget about your Grandmama.
If she don't come to visiting hours
the first week you're here, she don't want you back.*

I want my own clothes back.
My music. The food I like. I see the cars go by out there,
everybody goin someplace. In here, hours
stretch out long, nothin but blank white
walls to look at. I started a letter: *Dear Grandmama,
get me out of here . . .* But then I stopped

and ripped it up. I know I shoulda stopped
drinkin that first time I got caught up, back
in seventh grade. I know everything Grandmama
would say about all this. I keep thinkin there
must be some way to make myself listen, some clear white
light I could shine into my mind those hours

when I can't see my way back
or forward, the hours I think even Grandmama
won't care if I stop livin.   These walls are *so white.*

—*Helen Frost*

"White Walls" is from a young adult novel titled *Keesha's House,* scheduled for publication in 2003 by Farrar, Straus & Giroux.

"I Look Around and Wonder" is in the voice of Harris, a boy who has been kicked out of his house upon telling his parents that he is gay.

I Look Around and Wonder

Harris
Another note in my locker today: *Die*
Faggot. Scrawled in thick marker, red,
on notebook paper ripped in half,
folded to fit through those little slots.
Then later, someone twice my weight shoves me
into a table in the cafeteria. My lunch

goes flying, hits this freshman eating lunch
by herself. She looks like she's about to die,
like she thinks she's the jerk, not him. I apologize, she ignores me,
moves to another table, her face bright red.
There's so many guys like him — they have these slots
they try to fit you into; anyone with half

an ounce of individuality gets crushed. Kids spend half
their time just trying to fit in. You look around the lunch
room and you can see which kids are trying for which slots —
jocks or freaks or "playas." And everyone would rather die
than be what I am. Even the thugs, wearing red
or blue, with all their drugs and guns, have more friends than me.

Do people think I'm contagious? That if they talk to me
they might turn gay? Or are they scared that half
the school would hate them too? I've read
statistics: Maybe one in ten kids in that lunch
room. I look around and wonder. Kids can die
a lot of different ways if they don't fit in those slots.

Three more months of school. There's lots
of things I have to figure out. So far, Dad hasn't found me
and taken back my car. It's old, but with any luck it won't die
on me. If I can find someplace to park and sleep, that's half
the battle. I'll find a weekend job where I can get lunch,
and try for dinner shift on weekdays, work as many hours as I can. I read

an ad that Pancake House is hiring. I can see myself in that red
apron, pockets filling up with tips. Come summer, I can work whatever slots

they need — graveyard one day, lunch
the next, whatever.   Only — how can they call to offer me
a job? Can I clean up and look half
decent for an interview? And not sound desperate, like I'll die

if they don't hire me? I'll go on Saturday at lunch time, see what slots
they're trying to fill. Even half time, bussing their red
tables, would be something. I may be scared, but I don't plan to die.

—Helen Frost

"I Look Around and Wonder" is from a young adult novel titled *Keesha's House*, scheduled for publication in 2003 by Farrar, Straus & Giroux.

8
Nonfiction

Students often like to write nonfiction stories because it seems easier to write down what really happened than to invent plot and characters or come up with images. But, of course, they will discover that the lines between genres aren't clearly drawn. The kinds of images developed in writing poems enliven a fiction or nonfiction story, and real-life characters or events can serve as models for poetry and fiction.

In this chapter I suggest several short, relatively neutral activities, which allow, but don't specifically invite, students to write about difficult memories or experiences. These are followed by a longer writing activity, in which students are specifically invited to write about an experience of violence in their lives.

Remember a Specific Moment

This activity invites students to slow down a particular moment so that they can see inside it. That can be helpful in gaining emotional control of whatever happened. I often use poems as examples in this activity, even if the students are writing prose, because poems often get at the intensity of a particular moment. "The Portrait," by Stanley Kunitz (p. 52), is an example you could use. Here is another example, written by a student:

Trouble

I heard him calling me names.
I didn't want to get in trouble.
We started to yell at each other.
I didn't want to get in trouble.
I went to walk away. He put his hand on my shoulder.
I didn't want to get in trouble.
He spun me around. I heard the impact of my knuckles on his face.
I got in trouble.

—Hans

Begin by reading "The Portrait" (p. 52), "Trouble" (above), and "Pain" (p. 84), or select whichever example you feel is most appropriate for your class. Then ask students to describe a specific moment they remember. Tell them that it might be a happy or a sad memory, and it can be recent or from long ago. A few suggestions sometimes help students think of something to write about:

your first day of school, the first time you rode a bike, your first kiss

something you'll never forget or something you barely remember

something that happened after school yesterday

the first time you met someone you now know well

the birth of a person or an animal

the death of a person or an animal

something that makes you laugh or cry whenever you remember it

something you really wished for that came true or didn't come true

something that changed your life forever

something that happens every day, or once a week, or once a year, in just the same way

Be sure everyone has an idea (see Chapter 4) and has two sheets of paper and a pencil. Tell them that they will take notes on one piece of paper and then write about the memory on the second sheet of paper. Ask them to write down anything that comes to mind as you prompt them with the following suggestions:

- Go into the moment, in your mind. If this moment is sad or scary, enter it carefully, because writing about it could bring back some of those feelings.
- Look around you. What colors do you see? What is the smallest thing you see?

- Who is there?
- Is it night or day? Winter or summer?
- Take a deep breath. Do you smell anything? Can you describe the smell?
- Listen. Is anyone talking? Do you hear water running, or a dog barking, or traffic in the street? Are there any sudden noises that you didn't expect? What is the quietest sound?
- Describe the way you feel. You might want to compare the feeling to something else.
- Write down anything else that helps you remember the moment.

Give a minute or two for them to finish making these notes; tell them they don't have to answer each question, just use them to help recall the moment. Then ask them to simply describe the moment, starting fresh on a new sheet of paper and referring to their notes for details to make the writing more vivid.

Figure 8–1   A middle school student focuses on a difficult moment.

Trouble

I heard him calling me names.
I didn't wont to get in trouble
We started to yell at each other.
I didn't wont to get in trouble
I went to walk away.
He put his hand on my sholder
I didn't wont to get in trouble
He spun me around I heard the impact of my knuckles on his face.
Then I got in trouble

BY Hans.

Figure 8–2   An elementary student remembers a sad time.

Describe a Person You Know

Read Emily's story "True Courage" (p. 86) and either Jeff Gundy's story "'The Universe Is a Safe Place for Souls'" (p. 90) or Ketu Oladuwa's story "I Remember Mrs. King" (p. 88). All of these stories have details that bring a particular person to life in a particular time and place. Ask students to think of someone who has been important to them. It can be someone they met once or someone they see every day, someone they love or someone they don't like (remind them, though, of the rule that their writing cannot hurt anyone). A few ideas:

parents, grandparents, siblings, cousins, aunts, uncles

the oldest person you know

the youngest person you know

someone brave

someone mean

someone who confuses you

a teacher or a coach

a friend or an enemy

Someone usually asks if it can be an animal and I say, "Sure, if you can make the animal seem real and important." If I am asked if it can be someone famous (or God or Jesus), I suggest that they stick to someone they have met in person.

In a presentation similar to the previous activity, ask questions to prompt them to recall details:

How does this person walk? Compare his or her walk to something.

Describe this person's physical appearance.

What does this person wear when he or she is at home, relaxing?

What does this person do to relax?

What does this person wear when he or she goes to a grocery store?

What would this person buy at the grocery store?

Write one thing this person has said.

Describe a particular gesture that this person makes.

Write one thing this person has done.

Ask students to use their second sheet of paper to describe the person so that someone who has never met him or her would know what the person is like. Suggest that they include a particular moment that will let their reader know something important about the person.

Describe a Place Where Something Happened

Sometimes students really want to write about something specific that happened to them, but it feels threatening to actually say what happened. A relatively safe alternative is to think about something that happened, but instead of describing the event itself, just describe the room or the place where it happened. Students seem to find this activity satisfying in itself, but it can also lead to a longer or more complex piece of writing, either fiction or nonfiction.

Begin by reading the following poem:

My House

My house is big and warm with delight,
but has a huge gap because of the loss of my dad.
It smells like him and feels like he was there
but you know that he's not
and you'll always have a gap.

—Trever

Next, read "Sap" (p. 91), by Beth Simon. Put the Details of the Senses worksheet (p. 131) on an overhead. Ask for details from "Sap" that would fit in each place.

Then ask students to describe a place they know using this kind of physical detail. Offer some ideas of places to write about:

a place you feel safe

a place you were scared

a kitchen

a classroom

a basement

someplace outdoors

a place you haven't been to for a long time

your grandparents' house

Give each student a copy of the Details of the Senses worksheet. Ask them to imagine that they are in the place they have chosen to write about, and to write down details that describe the place, using as many of their senses as they can. "Sixth Sense" just means something they feel or know but can't quite say why or how. Using the notes they make on the worksheet, have them write a description of the place. They can enter and leave the place, or they can stay there throughout the story.

Write About a Personal Experience of Violence

A major writing project about any given topic takes a lot of time and commitment, but it can be valuable to you and your students and important to your community. The topic I discuss here is "how violence affects young people," but a similar approach could be used to explore issues of teen pregnancy, drug use, gang involvement, racism, or other topics.

This activity is based on my experience in six high schools, gathering stories to be used as the basis for the play *Why Darkness Seems So Light*, some of which were later compiled in an anthology with the same title. The entire project was a powerful experience for all of the young people and adults who were involved: administrators, writers, teachers, actors, publisher, parents, audience members, and, as I continue to discover, readers, both youth and adults. I recall hundreds of particular moments and offer a few here:

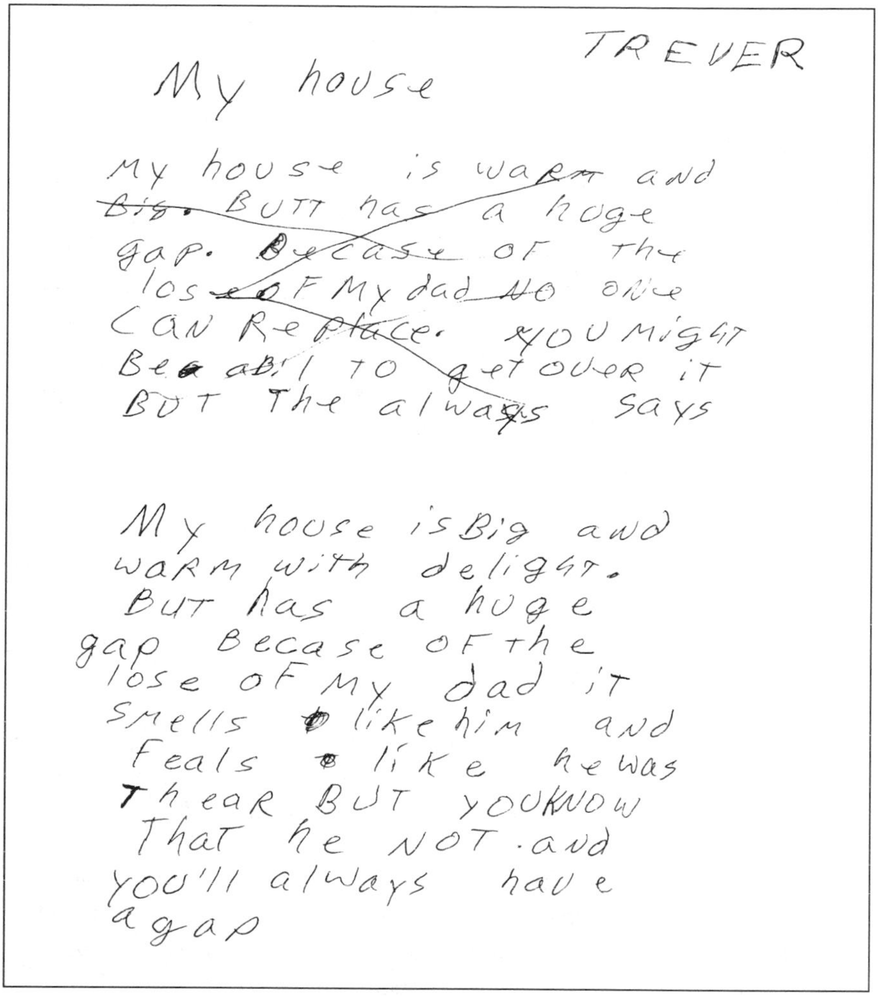

TREVER

My house

~~My house is warm and Big. BUTT has a huge gap. Becase of the lose of My dad No one can Replace. YOU Might Be abil TO get over it BUT The always says~~

My house is Big and warm with deligt. But has a huge gap Becase of the lose of My dad it smells like him and feals like he was thear BUT youknow That he NOT. and you'll always have a gap

Figure 8–3 A student uses six senses to describe his home.

A teacher tried to prepare me for meeting her classes. Her voice was weary as she described the high absentee rate, the students who came to class but fell asleep when they got there and never turned in their assignments. "They're there, but they're just marking time, and frankly, so am I. I'll retire in a year and a half, and I'm counting the days. I'm just telling you this so you won't be surprised if they don't write anything."

But they did write, and they wrote well, and they wrote a lot. When about a third of them put their heads down on their desks during my first day in the classroom, I said, "I don't think you're asleep, but it's hard for me to tell if you're listening when your heads are down. See if you can find a way to let me know if you can hear me." One student at a time, one eye at a time, they gave me that minimal acknowledgment I needed, and I went on speaking as if one eye, half-open, peeking above an arm, were an indication of rapt attention.

In a different school, a student appeared to be asleep as I talked about what we were doing, but then he started writing. He wrote nonstop for the entire three days I was in the classroom, and at the end of the third day, he handed me a long, poignant story about how and why his parents kicked him out of the house over a trivial argument. Just a few months later, I tried to contact him to ask permission to use his story in the anthology, and no one knew where he was.

I read many stories about events that I had first encountered in newspaper accounts over the previous seven or eight years: The first grader who had been sexually assaulted and murdered on her way home from school, remembered by the classmate who had shared a cubby hole with her. The thirteen-year-old, missing for three days and then found cut into pieces in a trash can, remembered by her next-door neighbor, who used to watch her walk across the lawn each morning. The young woman, shot when she was eight months pregnant with twins, remembered by her cousin, who was determined to love the one infant who survived. The church leader shot in her driveway, remembered by one of the youth group members who had gone on a field trip with her that weekend.

It went on and on, bringing to mind all the news stories and showing how many people are affected by each event. And then there were all the other acts of violence, unrecorded in the media but equally devastating to the children who survived them, many of whom had never had a chance to give their version of events or say how they felt about them.

Once the tap was opened, hundreds of stories poured out, astonishing the adults who received them and, as many students observed, letting the young people know that they weren't the only ones who had experienced violence.

If you would like to try something like this in your classroom, here are some specific suggestions as to how to go about it:

Before you introduce this activity in your classroom, define the context for it. Has there been an incident of violence in your community or on the national news? Have your students been reading about violence or discussing it? Has one of your students been a victim of violence, leaving others angry and grief-stricken? What reason do you and your students have for writing about this issue?

Send a note home to parents, letting them know what you are doing and how their child's writing will be used.

Take your time with this activity. Begin by asking your students to think of a time when they have witnessed or participated in an event in which violence was significant. Tell them that if they have no experience of violence (wonderful on the few occasions it happens), they can write about a situation in which a conflict was solved nonviolently. Here is a fairly typical list of what students in one high school class, of mixed socioeconomic background, in a mid-size American city, chose to write about:

neighbor raped and murdered

friend killed at party

mother murdered by stepfather

drunk boyfriend rips head off stuffed animal

mother chooses husband over kids—kicks writer out of house over minor argument

fight at football game—lots of "language"

walking away from fight

calling police about Dad's drug abuse—concern for younger children

father upset about mother's new boyfriend—fight when he comes to pick up kids

two men break into house in middle of night, looking for mom's boyfriend

fight on first floor of high school

cruelty to trapped animal

fights at middle school

fight at a party—fifty cars outside, big city

Figure 8–4   The author of "How One Night Changed My Life Forever"
(p. 84) suggests how you might help students write their stories.

Do you have any advice for teachers who are trying to help their students write about difficult things in their lives?

Tell the students to think of the most tradgetic thing that has ever happened to them.

Express all of what they had felt.

living with a violent father — hits mom and kids, mom gets restraining order

father hitting wife, kids — older child (writer) tries to protect younger ones

kids chased on bikes, get away, never go back to that street

writer teased about first pair of glasses — parents tell her she's pretty

little girl comes to the door to ask for food

friend's father interrupts phone conversation with unreasonable questions

fight at school broken up by conflict mediators

friend's head bashed to floor twenty times, brain damage — five girls against two

argument turns to fight, relatives

fight on school bus — role of instigators

parents fighting, think child (age 4 or 5) is upset about it, never fight again

fight over drug deal, parking lot

Take a few minutes to define violence and discuss the comparative magnitude of, for example, the murder of a loved one within the past year and a war in a distant country. Some students may argue that the war is worse because lots of people are killed, while others may feel that the proximity of an incident is what gives it importance. Some may feel that verbal violence can be just as hurtful as physical violence, while others may think that violence has to leave physical scars.

The discussion itself is as useful as any definition, but if you want to offer a comprehensive definition, I like this one, used by the Center for Nonviolence in Fort Wayne, Indiana: "Violence: any words or actions that hurt, scare, disrespect or control someone." Its definition of nonviolence is "Speaking up for the truth in ways that don't hurt." You can use that definition to point out how the serious writing they are doing differs from gossip about who is fighting whom and also differs from songs and movies that use violence for purposes of entertainment.

Now read aloud several examples of nonfiction stories, both adult and student. Some you could use are "I Remember Mrs. King" (p. 88), "How One Night Changed My Life Forever" (p. 84), " 'The Universe Is a Safe Place for Souls' " (p. 90), and "Pain" (p. 84).

Say that the experience they write about should be real life, not a story from TV or a movie or something they have read. They should not change details to make themselves look better or to make the story more dramatic, but they can do whatever they need to do in order to feel safe telling the story. Some safety measures might be:

changing all the names and enough details so we won't recognize the event

writing anonymously or using a pseudonym (If you give this option, you can't really grade any of the students.)

writing for the teacher's eyes only, requesting that the story not be shown to anyone else

Ask students to get out two pieces of paper and something to write with. Be sure everyone has an idea of what to write about (see Chapter 4). Ask students to give an overview, in one or two phrases or sentences, of what they are going to be writing about. For example:

the time my neighbor shot at my dog

the party when my friend got shot

One time my brother kicked me in the back and told me if I told Mom he'd beat me up worse. I never told anyone, but I've been scared of him ever since.

that time in seventh grade when a kid had a gun in school all day

Give one or two minutes for students to write this overview. Then say, "On the rest of your first sheet of paper, don't write complete sentences; just write the details that come to your mind as I ask this series of questions." Read the questions from the Writing About Violence, Prewriting Worksheet (p. 132). Alternatively, you can photocopy the worksheet and pass it out, but when I do that, I still like to read the questions out loud in order to set a fairly quick pace and create the sense of a writing community. Again, remind the students that this is a tool to help them generate ideas, not a quiz on which they have to answer every question.

After your students have done this initial writing exercise, follow through with the suggestions in Part 2 as you help them develop, polish, and possibly publish this writing.

Someone always asks, "How long does this have to be?" and I never set a length limit. I say, "Longer than a sentence and shorter than a book," or "You are the only one who knows how long it will take to tell your story." By leaving this decision in the students' hands, you give them *authority* (they are the authors and they have authority) and free them from the pressure of having to fill a prescribed amount of blank paper. The paper is thus transformed into a trusted friend, receiving their words.

Some students will write long, detailed accounts (see Michelle's story, p. 84), while others will write something short (see Tony's story, p. 84). Don't underestimate the amount of courage and effort it takes to write a short vignette. Sometimes the shortest stories are the most powerful pieces. Your appreciation of them may embolden students to try something longer, more complex, or more ambitious.

When you finish a writing project such as this one, it is worth asking students how they felt about doing it. It may be the first time they have written about something important to them; they may have been surprised to discover that they wanted to do it or that they were willing to put forth the required effort. It may establish a new level of trust among the students and between you and many of them. Be attentive to all that and to how it changes your responsibility to one another.

Nonfiction Examples: Student Writing

PAIN

It all started with Mike and one of the kids who rushed us. I don't know how it started. I don't really remember how it ended. I just remember pulling this dude off Mike, and then punching him in his throat and him falling to his knees. Then I kicked him in his stomach. He folded up after that.

I looked at my friends and myself beating these kids. Then the kid at my feet tried to get up. I snapped back in and started to kick in his face.

After we ran and got to Joe's house, we were hyped and glad. But that night I thought hard before I fell asleep. I thought if that was me? If that was my pain, and what was the reason for fighting?

— Tony

HOW ONE NIGHT CHANGED MY LIFE FOREVER

October 19, 1996 is a day I will never forget for as long as I live.

It was a warm autumn night in a city where I used to live, in Ohio. Everything started around 7:00 p.m. It was a Saturday night, and the day before, my best friend, Tyrone, got a new car. I had heard about a party on the "West Side" of town. I brought it up to Tyrone and he said he didn't want to go, simply because we lived on the East Side. He thought that it wouldn't be a good idea for the "Easts" to be going to a "Wests" party. All he kept saying was "No. Hell, no."

I begged and begged. It finally got on his nerves so he gave in and said "yes" but only until 12:30 a.m. I was so excited to go. I threw on my new outfit, which I will never forget. My new white Tommy shirt, with my new jeans, and of course my all white Nikes. I was so excited to go out with Tyrone and go to a West Side's party.

We finally left and we were on our way. It was about a 20-minute drive. It seemed like it lasted forever. Tyrone kept saying, "You know we shouldn't go. You know your dad will be mad if he finds out it's out west."

All I could say was, "Shut up, everything's fine. We ain't got nothing to worry about." Ignoring the bad feeling about the whole thing, I didn't care. I just wanted to go. Tyrone said, "If anything happens it's your fault."

When we arrived at the party, we heard music playing and people laughing and yelling and all I could think was "Yes, we are here!" I looked over at Tyrone. He was looking underneath his seat for his 9mm. His gun. And I yelled, "Damn it, Ty, put that away. Someone could see you with that. You won't even need it."

Feeling bad, he looked at me and said, "Sorry," and put it back underneath the seat.

We got out of the car and we immediately recognized our friends from our neighborhood, sitting on the front porch. Greetings were exchanged with a few handshakes representing our neighborhood "EAST" and throwing up the gang sign. That's what started the whole thing.

That night changed my life forever. I never imagined the outcome. I never even stepped a foot in the party.

Tyrone and I sat down to talk to our friends on the front porch. An all black Jeep Cherokee with black tinted windows pulled up across the street. The people in the Jeep just sat there for a few minutes. The driver rolled down the window and said "Ain't y'all from East?"

Ty's friends quickly yelled, "Yeah . . . why, who wants to know?"

The driver jumped out of his seat and ran over to us. Words were exchanged from the two sides. The guys from the Jeep ran over to Tyrone and his friends. All I could do was sit there hoping someone wouldn't get hurt, and frantically yelling, "Stop!"

Tyrone was in the middle of the street, fighting with some guy. The guy was short and cocky, very muscular. He looked really mean. He just looked at Ty with the evilest eyes and kicked him in the stomach. All Tyrone could do was lie on the ground. He kept trying to get up but he couldn't get up to his knees. Ty finally got up and bum-rushed the man. The guy got really mad and reached into his pocket and pulled out his gun.

Everything stopped. Everyone's eyes were on the guy (now the gunman). Everything was frozen. I could hear the trees rustle in the breeze and the ice cream truck across the street. Then there was a loud pop. Everyone ducked to hide. Tyrone stood there holding his chest. I looked around. All his friends ran.

"Tyrone," I screamed, "He's been shot! Call 911!" I ran over to hold Tyrone in my arms. Looking into his eyes, I could see fear like I have never seen before. It scared me.

There was blood everywhere. It ran down the street gutter like rain water and rolled down the sewer. It seemed like forever until the ambulance finally showed. I heard the sirens and said, "Baby, it's gonna be OK. Trust me."

He looked at me and said, "Please don't cry. It's gonna be OK." As soon as the paramedics came over, his eyes shut and his body fell limply. All I could do was scream and cry.

To this day, I still feel guilty, even after going through therapy for almost two years. It all would've changed and been better if I just hadn't asked.

I'm sorry Ty. R.I.P. I love you.

—*Michelle*

TRUE COURAGE

My little sister Amy is one of the most exasperating sisters alive, but she is also one of the strongest people I know. She is the typical junior high girl. She loves to look for cute guys with her friends, go to movies, watch unintelligent shows, and read teenybopper magazines. Yet she has to deal with more things than any average teenager.

She has severe medical and emotional problems, all which resulted from her birth parents. Her problems make living with her very difficult, but even on those days where I would love to sell her to the Gypsies I know that I have a rare and precious gift in my little sister, for she has taught me more about not giving up than any famous person or story ever could.

She entered my world on a gray August evening. My mom had just started foster care and she and her older brother were to be her first case. Later we would learn that none of the experienced foster mothers would take them because of their severe problems. My father, having been at work, did not know of their arrival and had been planning to take my mom out for a surprise dinner; instead he was the one with the surprise. My sister arrived at four months of age and her brother arrived at a little over two years. She was wrapped in a pastel knit rainbow blanket and he wore a red T-shirt and shorts. She was half-starved to death and he had survived by eating dog food. Both were severely traumatized. Her little baby belly was swollen, while the rest of her body was nothing but bruised skin on tiny little bones. Her parents had named her Shasta after the root beer, while her brother was named Rickie. Rickie was so traumatized that he wouldn't talk and he would go into fits of rage. Because he was so frightened by the past, all my mom could do was hold him and wait for her love and security to kick in.

I was so thrilled at the prospect of a baby and a little kid in my house that it took a while for me to understand that something was terribly wrong. Years passed and it became apparent that Rickie needed to be an only child in a loving home. Even though we loved him, he couldn't stay with us. So off he went to his new home, as we struggled to try to mend a broken child.

She was handicapped with cerebral palsy and with attention deficit disorder (ADD). Even though she was taken out of the abusive home at four months, she still had to go back for "supervised" visits. In short, the visits were not supervised and she was still abused. Finally, the visits were stopped, and when she was three we were finally able to adopt her. She needed counseling and therapy for her emotional and physical problems. Her doctors believe that my sister was born left handed but the right side of her brain was damaged so much that she had to become right handed. If you look at her writing it looks like you're writing with the hand that you normally wouldn't write with. She has the handwriting of a kindergartner even though she is in junior high. She has to work very hard to write anything legible; her hand shakes and her mind is working overtime just to write a simple letter. Most of her teachers see a troubled and unintelligent, obnoxious child, but it is to the contrary. She is a wonderful, smart, and loving child.

She is a people person. She has no trouble meeting and talking to people. I wish that I had her gift for people. I wish that I was able to greet people and make them feel so welcome in an instant with a smile and a word of encouragement. She forgives so easily, while I do not. Once a girl made fun of how she looked, but instead of crying or being mean, she looked at her and complimented her on her outfit. Not many people can be so gracious to those who persecute them. I couldn't, not as quickly as she can be.

Her teachers see her as unintelligent because it is hard for her to focus. They don't see past the brain damage to who she is or what she can be. It is hard for her to convey her ideas to them. While school is easy for me, she struggles and may be smarter than me. For she has the will, strength, and compassion that I never had until I was older. She is obnoxious, but no more than any other typical junior high girl, yet she isn't typical. She is strong and she will survive. At dinner you watch her pouring a jug of milk and her hand shakes so badly that you think that she is going to spill the entire jug all over, but she does not spill one drop. She has overcome abuse, emotional and physical pain, and learning disorders, to get to where she is today. To get to be my loving and lively little sister Amy.

— Emily

Adult Writing

I REMEMBER MRS. KING

Me and mama used to listen to a radio program late in the forties and early fifties called "I Remember Mama." Mama was there for me at an early age, but from the fourth grade on, it's Mrs. King that I remember.

Mrs. King, a petite blond with brown roots, hard, little blue eyes, and a biting sarcasm, was the fourth grade teacher who gouged out a hunk of my self-esteem, and took any sense of privacy I had at eight years old. Now, at fifty-five, I'm still recovering, and while one incident involving Mrs. King indelibly claws at my childhood memory, I understand now how time and place tuned my feelings on a balmy autumn day early in 1953.

I was a foster kid. My parents were paid to keep me, and though the love I got and learned there saved my life, the shame of not growing up with my parents like other kids, for a long time kept me terrorized about people finding out that my mama wasn't my mama.

I grew up about twenty miles north of New York City, in Westchester County, early in the Eisenhower years. The suburban boom hadn't yet happened in Westchester County. It hadn't yet become the bedroom capitol of New York City. Then, Westchester was still "upstate" and "country." I remember hog butcherings, turkeys and chickens being plucked and dunked in tubs of hot water, picking ripe fruit in the orchard and vegetables from the garden acre. There were pheasants dancing under the old oak tree in our front yard, and foxes cavorting in early evening at the hedgerow in the back, but most of all, I remember Mrs. King.

Mrs. King believed in Mrs. King. In her classroom, you dotted all the i's and crossed all the T's her way. One minute she'd be laughing and smiling with the students, and in the next, that witch would break into barely controllable sobs that left us students stunned. But my most perplexing moments in the fourth grade came when Mrs. King turned her wrath on me. She would cut her eyes at me as if to tell the butcher that I was meat to be hacked up. Intimidated? Yeah, I was scared of Mrs. King!

Adrienne and I were the only black kids in a class of about twenty-five on the first day of school. Adrienne was real fair-skinned, with wavy auburn hair that didn't have to be straightened to "be good." I was dark complexioned with every nap of my hair standing alone. I stood out like a "fly in a sugar bowl."

Before silencing the class to give out seating assignments, Mrs. King looked at me with a disgust that knotted in my stomach. By the time she read my name, my hands were sweating and I couldn't sit still. My seat was in the corner at the back of the room. Seating assignments were alphabetically arranged. My name came before Adrienne's and about twelve or thirteen other kids in class, but I was placed in the back of the class. Adrienne was in the front row. I didn't really understand all of this then. I felt kind of at ease being far away from Mrs. King.

I raised my hand to go to the bathroom. "And what do you want?" she asked, not looking at me. "What do you want?" she half shouted. Without ever looking at me, she finally waved me off, and I ran to relieve myself.

When I returned from the bathroom, I quietly took my seat. Mrs. King was explaining that we would be going on a field trip to the Statue of Liberty in New York City. We were to bring a permission slip back to school the next day, signed by our parent. Mrs. King didn't pay me any attention the rest of the day. Although I knew answers to questions she asked, and I furiously waved my hand to be called on, she always overlooked me. One time no one else knew the answer, and she just acted like she never saw me. She did scold me for day-dreaming.

I didn't say much to Mama about school, except that I didn't like the teacher. It'd be all right, she told me. I took the permission slip back to school the next day. It was really a nice day, and I was happy. Mrs. King greeted the class good morning. We said the Pledge of Allegiance, and sang America the Beautiful. Then Mrs. King took the roll and collected the permission slips. Going over them she noticed the names of some children's parents that she evidently knew. When she got to my slip, her face changed to a puzzled look. Then she looked at me.

"Who signed this slip for you?" she asked.

"My mom," I said.

"Your mom?" she hesitated. "This is signed by someone named Taylor. Your name's not Taylor. Who signed this slip?"

Again, I answered, "my mom," but this time with more urgency and conviction.

"No," said Mrs. King. "You're lying! How can this be your mother? You don't have the same name. Why don't you have the same name as your mother?"

I couldn't say anything at first. I wanted to crawl under the desk. My face felt like it was on fire. Tears were rolling down my face. "I don't know," I whispered. "She's my mama and she takes care of me and other children."

"Oh," says Mrs. King, "you mean you're a foster child." The class, which already was looking at me with amazement, then began to snicker and laugh. Mrs. King made light of the incident. "Oh, all you had to do was say you were a foster child."

Mrs. King didn't know how ashamed I was of who I was. Mrs. King didn't know I felt that I wasn't good enough to live with my birth parents. I was different in ways that I could never fix, and now everyone knew. I spent forty years trying to fix myself before I found out I wasn't broken.

— Ketu Oladuwa

Ketu Oladuwa is a student of life who writes and plays music as a prelude to human interaction. The practice maintains a balanced character. He writes this about "I Remember Mrs. King":

I thank Mrs. King for being a superb teacher. She taught me early to never trust people who purposely hurt me.

"THE UNIVERSE IS A SAFE PLACE FOR SOULS" *FOR JIM SARGENT*

All right then. So what about Gary Eden, my archenemy all through junior high and the last person I ever fought in the serious physical sense? He was the best athlete in our class, but being a north-of-town Lutheran he got into hot cars and beer and never went out for anything after eighth grade. He wasn't all that vicious, but blond, lean and good-looking in his simple way, and bigger, stronger, faster and dumber than I was.

For years off and on I went around in fear of his picking at me, stealing my basketball when we were shooting around before practice, snapping wet towels at me in the locker room, driving me near and beyond tears long after I thought I was too old for that. Finally once in the locker room he stopped and looked at me oddly and almost seemed to change. He held his hand out. Sorry, he said. Sure you are, I said. No, I mean it, he said. Sure, I said, and looked at his hand. Sure you are. We got dressed. After that we quit fighting. We never talked. We were not friends. I don't know now if he meant it or not.

— Jeff Gundy

Jeff Gundy is the author of four books of poetry and nonfiction, the most recent of which is *Rhapsody with Dark Matter*. He teaches at Bluffton College in Bluffton, Ohio. He writes this about "The Universe Is a Safe Place for Souls":

> What bothers me most about the situation in "'The Universe is a Safe Place for Souls'" is what I still don't know — about Gary, and about myself. Did he really mean to give up his petty bullying (not really much, as these things go)? Could we have been friends? Was I in some way as much a problem to him as he seemed to me? As these things go, I left for college thirty years ago and haven't really been back. I remember him being at a class reunion, but I still could not find anything to say to him, any way to break through the distance between us. Perhaps this story is my way of starting that process.

From *Flatlands*, by Jeff Gundy, 1995. Cleveland State University Poetry Center.

SAP

Good Friday, the conifers are rich in resin. A cemetery near my house hides a stand of long leaf and spruce.

Sly young girl, I sneak out of school, go home, make myself clean. I snag the old man's raveling cardigan off the back porch nail, wrap up like a secret, slip out through the root cellar, past the crabapple full of jays who suddenly cry my name. I enter the rutty field.

Lost in frost fog, head down in the dead brass of bean waste, dry wind fills my ear. My feet grow hard, cold, heavy, they rise, fall, rise on chalky furrows, jabbed by sharp-edged clods thrown in fall plowing.

Then, I'm across. Up the small hill. Emerge, sweaty, blown, at the graves. At the tree, the white pine, its harp body dark in thin sunlight. The lower branches swirl ground and I crawl under.

Dim. A held breath of cinnamon and rot. Around the base, a rug of needles, and I lie down, face to them, smooth as rice. I roll to one side and clutch a low bough. I trace its silk across my cheek. Again, then again, then curl to the trunk.

An amber rill has flowed down a crevice, congealed on a knee above the base. I press against the bark like earth, like mint. Lick. Nothing. I jab with my tongue, scrape pitch onto my teeth, and it is cold. Rank.

Such bitterness. My jaws snap shut. My mouth swells with saliva. I cannot swallow, cannot spit. Vegetal, animate, a deep unfamiliar life. Here is the heart.

—Beth Simon

Beth Simon divides her time between Fort Wayne, Indiana, and Madison, Wisconsin. She writes fiction, poetry, and essays. She teaches linguistics and creative writing at Indiana University/Purdue University. She writes this about "Sap":

The landscape of "Sap" is from my childhood memories and dreams of the west edges of Des Moines, Iowa, where I grew up—the fields of the truck farmers, the small rises and rivers.

"Sap" first appeared in *TriQuarterly* 90 (1994).

9
Fiction

Fiction can offer a safe way for writers to speak about whatever is on their minds. The pressure is off, in terms of revealing personal information, but if they want to, writers can invent characters who face similar problems to those they face themselves. Then they can take the time to invent plausible solutions for the characters, and that often helps them think through some of the difficult situations in their own lives. They also see that their life experiences have value as source material for fiction.

For the most part, take students at their word when they present something as fictional; don't assume that any story is autobiographical. If, however, a student writes something that causes concern—for example, Alyssa's story about suicide (p. 103)—pay attention, and talk to the writer about it, asking something like, "Do you want to tell me anything about how you got the idea for your story?" Responses to such a question will vary:

"No, I don't."
"It happened to me in fifth grade."
"It happened to my friend."
"I saw something like this on TV one time."

Be open to whatever students want to say about their stories, and let the stories themselves do most of the talking. Sometimes working on a story together offers a way for young writers to approach topics that are hard to talk about. In a fourth-grade classroom, children were writing a group story about a character whose parents were getting divorced, and they thought the story should say why. The reasons they suggested may give an idea of what kids worry about in such a situation, and each of the reasons suggests a plausible plot for a story:

"Probably it's because they don't have enough money."

"Their kid keeps on getting into fights."

"No, it's because the father hits the mother too much."

"Or maybe the mother just wants a different boyfriend."

"I think it's happening because they have too many kids."

"Maybe they both had kids when they got married, and the mother's kids don't get along with the father's kids."

In a different situation, when a group of teenage boys were discussing the poem "I Look Around and Wonder" (p. 71) they talked about Harris in a way that would have been impossible had they been discussing a real person or speaking directly about their own life experience:

"What made him get that way? I mean, you don't just wake up one day and say 'I think I'll go with guys.'"

"No, sometimes they do. My uncle was married and everything, and one day, he did that. He just left my aunt and started living with this dude."

"Well, I still think something happened to him. Somebody did something to him when he was little."

"Probably his uncle."

"No, it was his step-father."

"No, his neighbor."

"Maybe it was a friend of his older brother."

They went on in that vein for awhile, carrying on a serious conversation with a generally respectful tone, in sharp contrast to their usual bantering, in which any reference to being gay was expressed as an insult.

Many of the exercises and worksheets from the chapters on other genres may be adapted for use in writing fiction. Skill in describing people and places is as useful in fiction as it is in nonfiction. A sense of story and an ear for dialogue are essential to both drama and fiction writing—and to nonfiction and narrative poetry, as well. Knowing how to develop clear images will enhance any writing. But here are a few specific suggestions to help your students plan and develop stories.

Reading as a Writer

When your students read novels and short stories, in addition to other aspects of your discussion, encourage them to focus on what decisions the writer made as the story was written. This will make your students better writers as well as better readers. Make it an ongoing part of your classroom conversation, and then when students run into difficulties with their writing, suggest that they look carefully at a story they love and analyze how the author solved a similar problem.

For an example of the way a student might learn about writing by focusing on particular elements in a story, read the passage from *Oh My Darlin'*, by Claire Ewart (p. 104) to your students. Note how much Ewart shows us, in this short passage, about each member of the family as well as about the different relationships they have with one another. Pay attention to her use of physical detail to describe emotion. Notice how she *shows* how the characters feel instead of *telling* us directly.

Following are some questions you can use to guide a class discussion about this passage in a way that will help your students sharpen their writing skills. (You may wish to photocopy the excerpt and create handouts for students to refer to while discussing the writing.)

- What details help you answer the following questions: Where does the story take place? When does the story take place? How old are these characters? The answers to these questions aren't given in any exact way, but from reading this passage, we can make a good guess at all of them.
- Are the characters in this scene saying what they really feel? If you think they are feeling something other than what they are saying, what do you think they really feel? How does the author suggest that?
- What gestures does the author describe? What do these gestures tell you about the family relationships?
- For each of the four characters, make a list of all the verbs the author uses to describe his or her actions. What does this list tell you about the characters' emotions?
- Think about two images the author uses to describe the look on someone's face: "like he was lighting kindling among damp stones" (Pa) and "his suddenly glacial eyes" (Buddy). What do these images tell you about how the characters are feeling?
- As students work on their own stories, encourage them to ask similar questions about their own writing: Have you given your reader clues as to the age of your characters? Have you used details that suggest when and where the story takes place? Have you described gestures and used

verbs that indicate emotion? Have you used images or comparisons to make your writing more vivid?

Planning a Story: River of Choices

I adapted this from an exercise designed by staff at the Center for Nonviolence in Fort Wayne, Indiana, as a tool for helping young people think about choices in their own lives. I have used it to help students develop an idea for a fictional story.

First, make an overhead transparency of the River of Choices worksheet (p. 134) and enough photocopies for each student. Begin by doing this activity as a group exercise, writing on the overhead as the students suggest answers. See Figure 9–1 for a diagram of a group response that corresponds with the following example.

Figure 9–1   An example of a completed River of Choices worksheet.

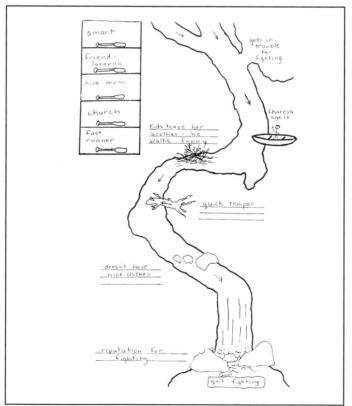

Introduce the activity by saying, "We're going to imagine a character who wants something to happen, but who faces obstacles along the way. The river represents the story; the character will be in the boat going down the river. Each of the oars represents something or someone who can help the character. The sticks and stones represent obstacles or problems the character faces."

Then talk about inventing the character: "Draw your character in the boat and write the character's name and age beside him or her. At the top of the page, write what is happening to the character when the story begins." In our example, the character, Charesa, age 12, gets in trouble for fighting.

Now talk about the goal: "In the box at the bottom of the river, write what Charesa wants to do or achieve." In our example, the character's goal is to quit fighting.

Next, explain the oars: "In each box above the oars, list something that could help Charesa. These could be her own good qualities or people who can help her." For example:

She's smart.

She has a good friend, Johanna.

Her mom's nice.

She goes to church.

She can run fast.

Discuss the obstacles: "At each obstacle along the way, write something about Charesa or something that happens to her that makes it hard for her to quit fighting." For example:

Pile of sticks: "Kids tease her little brother about how he walks funny."

Log: "She has a quick temper."

Boulders: "Everybody says her clothes are raggedy."

Rocks at the bottom: "She has a reputation as a fighter."

Now, develop the story. Say: "Let's imagine how this story might go." For example:

TEACHER: How should our story begin?

STUDENT: Start out with her getting in a fight.

STUDENT: Yeah, somebody says, "Charesa, how come your brother walks like a duck?" so she beats him up.

TEACHER: Then what happens?

STUDENT: She gets in trouble.

STUDENT: She has to stay after school, and her mom gets mad 'cause she has to leave work early to go pick her up.

STUDENT: No, we said her mom's nice.

STUDENT: Oh, yeah, her mom picks her up and has a little talk with her on the way home.

TEACHER: What would her mom say?

STUDENT: She might say, "Charesa, honey, did you get hurt?"

STUDENT: And then she'd give her some advice.

TEACHER: What advice?

STUDENT: Maybe like my dad says, "Don't beat up the same kid twice."

Continue to talk about the story as outlined on the diagram, but make it clear that you don't need to use every oar or include every obstacle. They are just ideas to help you develop a story.

Charesa's story might end up something like this:

A girl named Charesa was walking out of school one day with her little brother, Thomas, when a boy named Jeremiah shouted out, "Charesa, your brother walks like a duck!"

Charesa turned around fast, and before she thought about what she was doing, she punched Jeremiah in his face. He fell down, and Charesa was just about to kick him when the principal came out and said, "Charesa, you have to stay after school today."

Thomas took the bus home by himself, and he called their mom. She had to leave work early to take care of Thomas and pick up Charesa.

Charesa's mom was nice. When Charesa got in the car, her mom said, "Honey, did you get hurt?" and then she said, "Didn't you fight Jeremiah a couple weeks ago? Didn't I tell you — don't fight the same kid twice."

The next day, Charesa walked to school with her friend, Johanna. They saw Jeremiah coming toward them and he said, "Ha, ha. Look at Charesa. She's wearing her big brother's old jacket."

Johanna said, "Come on, let's just ignore him."

But Charesa was mad. She said, "Jeremiah, if I had a big brother, he would grind your ugly face up into dog food."

Jeremiah came after her. He never got a chance to get back at her the day before, and he wanted to try. But Charesa took off running. She beat Jeremiah to school and went inside before the bell rang.

The rest of the day, she didn't get in any fights. Her mom was so happy they got to have pizza for dinner that night.

It's a start. The exercise helps students start thinking about their characters and what might happen to them.

After composing one story as a whole-class activity, give each student a copy of the River of Choices worksheet and let them use it to help them think of an idea for a story of their own.

Guidelines for Writing a Story

The Fiction Writing worksheet (p. 135) will help your students begin writing their stories. It can be used in conjunction with the previous activity or as a separate exercise.

When your students are working on a story, give them enough time to explore, and tell them to expect to make a few false starts and sidetracks. Tell them not to worry if the story gets away from them and turns out differently than they had planned; when they finish, they can go back to the beginning and make it all fit together smoothly.

As your students are working, don't overwhelm them with rules or instructions. But, the following issues, in a vastly oversimplified form, are a few things writers should be aware of.

POINT OF VIEW

If you tell the story from the point of view of your main character, don't say anything about what other people are thinking. Just tell what your main character is thinking and observing.

You can either write about the character, using "he" or "she" even when you are telling what the character is thinking (see *Oh My Darlin'*, excerpt, p. 104, or "Almost Dead," p. 103), or write as if you are the character, using "I" even though the character is different from you, the author (see "Natonya's Night Wishes," p. 101, "Eat Dirt," p. 106, or my poems in the voices of young people, pp. 69 and 71).

VERB TENSE

You can write about the story as if it has already happened (past tense) or write about it as if it is happening right now (present tense). Stick with the same tense for the whole story, unless you make a conscious decision not to.

THE OPENING SCENE

Don't do too much explaining. Start right out with something happening, and add details to let your reader know who your characters are, where the story is happening, and what the problem is.

DIALOGUE

Find a story you love, and notice how good dialogue helps make it interesting. Imagine that you can hear your characters talking, and write down their exact words. Remember to start a new paragraph whenever someone starts talking. Follow an example from a book to learn how to punctuate dialogue.

KEEP WRITING

Let the first scene give you an idea about what happens next.

Write about that.

And then let *that* scene suggest the next one.

Don't solve the problem too quickly. Usually two or three things happen before the problem is solved. The problem in a story often gets worse before it gets better.

Create at least one scene in which the character is alone or with one trusted friend.

How does the character feel about what is happening?

THE ENDING

It doesn't have to be a happy ending, but there should be a sense that something has been settled or solved. Be sure your character solves his or her own problem. Don't have something happen to make the whole problem go away by itself. Don't have someone else solve the whole problem for the character. If someone helps, let your reader know how your character feels about that.

Editing and Polishing a Story

After you have a rough idea of what happens in your story, go back over it, working on each scene to see if you can bring it to life with details and dialogue. You might change the way things happen, or the names of characters, or other details. If you change something, make sure you change it throughout the story.

Pay attention to spelling and punctuation so that your readers will be able to understand what you mean.

READER RESPONSE

Share your story with one or two friends. Ask them to tell you if they are confused about anything, and if they are, see if you can find a way to make the story more clear. Adding detail is usually more effective than explaining everything.

FINAL COPY

Make a neat final copy. Illustrate it if you want to. Don't worry if you still want to change your story after you think it's finished. Lots of writers keep on changing things in their stories for a long time.

Fiction Examples: Student Writing

NATONYA'S NIGHT WISHES

Natonya thought that 13 was an unlucky number.

Me—I thought it was magical. I was nine and a half, and I couldn't wait until I would be a teenager.

Natonya was always angry because she had the same old friends, her face looked the same, and the boys still didn't notice her. Natonya decided maybe 13 was dumb.

Mama Dear came in. She was a country lady. She was Natonya's grandmom. "Why the long face?" she asked.

Natonya just sat there and looked out the window. Finally she went back out to her party to open up presents. The first one was a football. She looked around to see who gave it to her.

"Thanks, Andrew," she said with a sigh.

"What's wrong, Natonya?" asked her mom.

"Nothing," said Natonya, "I think I'm sick. I better go inside."

Her party still went on until 7:00 that night. After the party was over, I came in and there was a crack in our room door. From inside, I heard a voice. It was the voice of Natonya. "I wish I was a regular girl who had boyfriends, well, just one for now, and I wish I had a lot of friends."

I ran to Mom and told Mom. Mom said, "Kina, go to bed."

I prayed that night, just to make Natonya feel good, but that made her mad. I didn't understand her.

The next morning, I woke up and went to the bathroom. That's when I saw Natonya's hair in pigtails and her face all different colors. She had one of my dresses on which was too short, but she had it on. She had on Grandmom's alligator shoes and some lime green pantyhose.

I ran to Mom, but Mom said, "Girl, leave your sister be."

I went outside to feed our dog. Damion was our dog. He was evil. I was scared of him. I fed him four feet away from me. I practically threw his food to him.

Natonya was looking out the window. When I looked up, she quickly closed the blinds. I went in the house and ran upstairs to our room, but the door was locked. I got a bobby pin and picked the lock. Natonya was kissing her teddy bear, Mr. Bunts.

I ran to Mom. Mom said, "Girl, stop coming to me telling me lies."

I ran back to our room. Suddenly there was a knock on the door. It was DeMarcus, tossing a baseball in the air. DeMarcus would just run up to our room 'cause he was our cousin.

He saw Natonya's face and he dropped his ball. He said, "Dang, girl, what the heck happened to you?" Natonya slapped him and ran to the bathroom and changed her clothes.

After a long day of baseball, it was time for supper. Natonya and I walked home together. On the way home, she asked me silly questions like, "How does it feel to have a boy kiss you?"

I said, "How would I know?"

After eating spaghetti, I ran upstairs to take my bath and brush my teeth. When I walked in the room, Natonya was praying again. This time I heard her say, "God, I like this boy named James, but he don't know if I exist."

I ran to Mom. Mom said, "Go to bed, Kina."

I went in the room and Natonya was in the bathroom. On the bed, I found a sheet of paper. It said, "Natonya and James." When Natonya came in the room, she saw the paper had been moved. She hid the paper and went to sleep.

The next morning was Sunday. I got up and got ready for church. Natonya took her time in the bathroom. When she came out, she looked like a black American princess.

Mother came out after her with a pair of earrings, not just any kind, she had the dangly ones.

I asked Mom where were mine and she gave me a pair of small teddy bear ones.

While we were in church, I saw some new people there, and I noticed they had a son. He was staring at Natonya. I whispered to her, and she said, "Listen, fool."

After service, Mom went over to meet the family and what a surprise, their son's name was James!

"So, you're James," I said.

"Yes," he said. Natonya bumped into me, trying to keep my mouth shut.

James and Natonya walked by the old oak tree and I heard them talking about a baseball game. They sat on a huge boulder. They got closer and I saw a glow in their eyes.

They heard the bushes rattle, and they ran out from behind the tree.

Natonya caught up with me and said, "If you tell, I'll kill you."

Mom saw us and she said, "Get over here."

When we got over there, I said, "Mom, Natonya . . ."

And Mom cut me off and said, "Manners."

I waited until Mom got through talking. I decided to keep my mouth shut.

When we got home, I went in the room to change my clothes. Natonya decided to keep her church clothes on and go for a walk. I decided to follow her.

She met James at the baseball field. They were behind the bleachers, kissing.

I said, "Natonya! I'm telling!"

She chased me down and said, "I'll give you Mr. Bunts if you don't tell."

So I said, "OK."

When we got home, Natonya pulled a note from her pocket. She was in a haze, and on the cover it said, "James." Natonya ran upstairs and closed the door.

I took my bath and brushed my teeth and hair, and once again I heard Natonya in the room, wishing.

I ran to Mom. Mom said, "Girl, go to bed."

When I went back upstairs, Natonya was in the bathroom. She was singing. That's when I realized that Natonya was becoming a girl.

Natonya came in the room and she was trying on different dresses.

I didn't say nothing, and I acted as if I were sleeping.

Now I know why Natonya had night wishes.

— Erskina

ALMOST DEAD

She held the sharp, shiny, deadly object in her hand. Moving her finger up and down the blade, the blade she was planning to take her life with.

Although it was a beautiful day outside, she didn't notice. Her mind was concentrated on only one thing: her problems. Alone in her bedroom, she replayed the past few months of her life: her friends, her ex-boyfriend, her mom, everything that had gone wrong.

She thought of the day, not long ago, when she and her best friend had had their first fight. That had also been a beautiful day, but because of her anger and stubbornness, she hadn't noticed.

She sat there feeling the blade of her knife, going over in her mind what it would be like with no problems. Alone. Dead. Her heart was beating faster than it had ever gone. She was more nervous than she had ever been.

Although she hadn't said good-bye to anyone, she had written a note to her mom and her best friends, and a poem for her ex-boyfriend. She knew they would understand. Her confidence was at a high just as the sun set.

She didn't know how long she had been sitting there, but she knew she was ready. She wanted to test the waters, so she made a small incision on her left wrist. She felt nothing but relief. She felt no pain or hurt, only relief. She made another small incision and sat there watching her arm slowly bleed.

The cuts were not deep enough to kill her, but now she knew she could make the final cuts, the cuts she hoped would finally put her out of her life of misery, her days of tears.

She felt a tear slide down her cheek; she hadn't noticed, but she was crying again. She closed her eyes and started to think of all the days she had cried, and remembered the days when she hadn't.

Then she felt something brush against her leg. She opened her eyes to see her cat. Her cat was eight years old, and hardly ever allowed anyone to pet her. Yet, right then, her cat was looking for affection. Her cat lay down in her lap, purring.

For the first time in months, she smiled. Instead of rubbing her knife, she started rubbing her cat. She felt something she hadn't felt in awhile — love, need, warmth. After petting her cat for half an hour, she realized she didn't want to die. She wanted her problems to go away, her friend and her to make up, but she really didn't want to die.

She will always have the small scar marks from the incisions to remind her of what happened. But she promised herself, and her cat, that she would never, ever, try or think of committing suicide again.

—Alyssa

Alyssa wrote this story in high school, and she is in college now. She writes this about "Almost Dead":

This story is a fictional and also a nonfictional story. The events are memories of mine but some of the ideas are not real.

Adult Writing

This excerpt from Claire Ewart's novel comes early in the story and tells us a lot about Clemma and her family and where they all live.

OH MY DARLIN'

Then one day when Clemma got off the bus after school, an important-looking envelope was waiting in the mailbox. It was addressed to Buddy. Hurriedly, Clemma skipped across the cattle guard and carried the envelope to the house. Buddy was in the kitchen scouring the rust off a pair of old spurs.

"Here Bud. It's for you!" Clemma handed Buddy the letter with an important flick of the wrist.

"So it says . . ." Buddy put the spurs down, his hands not moving from the table.

"Come on . . . open it!" Clemma pulled herself up onto the counter by the sink. She sat there swinging her legs.

Buddy didn't say a word. He turned the envelope in his stained hands, smudging it, not opening it.

"Come on Bud!" Clemma whined. What's the matter with him? she wondered.

Just then Pa came into the kitchen.

"What cha got there?" Pa scratched his chin, in need of a shave. He leaned over the table, over Buddy.

"Here, Pa." Buddy swallowed. He handed Pa the envelope.

Pa tore into it, and for a moment his face went still. Then, like he was lighting kindling among damp stones, the corners of his mouth lit into a pasted-on smile.

"Louisa, your son's going to be a soldier!" Pa called to Mama, who was in the living room.

"Oh Bud!" Clemma breathed. Her heart thumped over. Now she understood. Hand grasping for anything, she grabbed for the letter. There it was all spelled out. Buddy was ordered to report to Basic Training. . . . Just like Pa said, Buddy was going to be a soldier. He was going to be sent to Vietnam.

Clemma looked at Buddy, his suddenly glacial eyes, the smudges of rust and oil on his long-fingered hands, the way the russet hair fell carelessly across his forehead. Wasn't he just a boy? How could they take him to be a soldier?

Buddy looked right back, like he had something he wanted to say just to her, but instead he took the letter and crumpled the edge, and turned to stare out the window.

"You'll be like your Pa I expect." That's what Mama said as her feet scuffed the linoleum coming into the kitchen. She brushed a strand of graying hair behind her ear.

Clemma noticed Mama's cheek quivering. She wasn't smiling.

"Oh Bud!" Clemma said again and bit her lip. There had to be some mistake.

"You'll make us proud. . . . Stand up to those Commies," Pa slapped Buddy on the back. "No coward draft dodger in this family!" Like he was making sure Buddy understood, Pa kept his hand square between Buddy's shoulders.

Clemma saw Buddy close his eyes under the weight.

Mama, her eyes set and pale, her hand shaking ever so slightly, brushed Buddy's hair from his face.

Clemma just sat.

—Claire Ewart

Claire Ewart is the author and illustrator of many children's books, including *One Cold Night*. Her work has appeared on the PBS television program *Reading Rainbow*. She lives in Fort Wayne, Indiana. She writes:

> *Oh My Darlin'* is about difficult choices and doing what we think we must. This passage gives us a sense of the shock, bravado, and misgivings experienced by Clemma's family when her brother Buddy is ordered to go to Vietnam to the war.

This excerpt is from *Oh My Darlin'*, a novel-length manuscript.

EAT DIRT

Say you never ate dirt? You're a plain fool.

All the good things dirt got in it. Full of grit. Now, who can't use some? Don't be making faces at me. I know what I'm talking about.

Dirt got sunshine in it. Years on end of light in a mouthful.

And dead folks is in the dirt, just a-talking and a-dancing. Swallow some, and they'll tell you things. You'll get a old folks mind in a young folks heart. Help you step clear of trouble.

And moles gone through the dirt so the dark won't feel strange to you no more.

Don't look at me funny. Better take your ears out your pockets and listen. Dirt got God's tears in it.

Me, I eat dirt regular. Every other day. It grows sweet corn and trees big as houses. Just think what it'll do for you. Better eat you some dirt, honey, and see what it grows in you.

—Constance García-Barrio

Constance García-Barrio, a Philadelphia freelance writer, teaches at West Chester University in Philadelphia. She writes this about "Eat Dirt":

> This story was inspired by Rose Ware, my great grandmother, who was born into slavery about 1851, and lived to be 113. Her life was close to the earth and I believe she helped me with this story.

First published in *Kerf Literary Review*, June 1998.

10
Drama

I love the sound of the human voice. My father's trilled *r*s (a remnant of the Norwegian language spoken in his early childhood), my aunt's insistence that the word *beautiful* has four syllables, the cadences of conversation among a multicultural group of teenagers talking to one another when they don't think I'm listening — such rich music all around me.

Young people are immersed in such language, and they can be taught to recognize and write down the dramatic elements of it. Because most of them are familiar with movies and television, and some have experience with stage productions, they have a sense of theatre, and they can learn how to frame a scene in writing.

Try writing a dramatic scene yourself. Recall, in detail, a public or private event. Do you remember:

- your first day of junior high
- a time you got in trouble
- the death of someone close to you
- a time when you felt betrayed or when you betrayed someone
- a difficult decision
- any personal memories about President Kennedy's assassination, the Challenger explosion, the Oklahoma City bombing, or local news events
- something that happened when you were the age your students are now

Choose one of those memories and frame it in a particular time and place. Do a quick freewriting exercise to see if you can re-create the scene, defining it through setting, characters, and dialogue. For example, maybe there was a food fight in the school cafeteria in seventh grade:

- First, define the setting. Imagine a stage set or an opening shot in a movie. Example: A long cafeteria table, eight kids on each side. Sounds of scraping feet, banging trays, laughing and shouting.
- Next, choose your characters. Use real names in this freewriting. (If you develop this piece of writing, or show it to anyone else, you will probably want to change the names later on.) Give a brief description of each character. Example:

  Melissa (smart, a little annoying, everyone teased her about her acne)
  Kent (thought he was God's gift to girls)
  Janet (really, really wanted to fit in)
  Kenny (short and cute, girls treated him like a teddy bear)
  Mrs. Watson (social studies teacher on lunch duty, high-pitched angry voice)

- Think of which two or three characters are most important to the scene. They will have the most lines in your script. Example: Kent, Janet, Mrs. Watson
- Decide where the scene begins. Example: Everyone is eating peacefully when Kent flicks a spoonful of mashed potatoes at Kenny, but it misses and hits Janet.
- Write a page or two of dialogue with parenthetical descriptions of actions.

Leaving these seventh graders alone with Mrs. Watson for the moment, write this scene from one of your own memories. Use one of the scenes from *Why Darkness Seems So Light* (pp. 114 and 116) as a model for format and punctuation.

You will see how much you do remember and how much you don't. Voices will come back to you, as well as cadences of speech, varying tones of voice, slang terms, and gestures. Put these memories together and use your imagination to fill in what you don't remember.

Now you're ready to present a similar activity to your students. Begin by either putting one of the scenes from *Why Darkness Seems So Light* (pp. 114 and 116) on an overhead so that your students will have a sense of how a dramatic scene appears on the page. Then encourage them to think of something that really happened to them and write it as a script, changing names and details as necessary in order to feel safe and to protect others.

Next, teach or review with them what a setting is, using examples from any genre: the home for unwed mothers in "Watermelon Hill" (poem, p. 68), the kitchen in the excerpt from *Oh My Darlin'* (fiction, p. 104), Rose's living/dining room in Scene 5 of *Why Darkness Seems So Light* (drama, p. 114) the locker room in "'The Universe Is a Safe Place for Souls'" (non-fiction, p. 90).

Talk about how we define characters and what is essential for us to know. Generally we need to know the name, the age, and the gender of each character as well as the characters' relationships to one another. Talk about the decision as to whether race or ethnicity should be a defining characteristic; this will vary for each student's script.

Discuss styles of speech. Would the characters be speaking formally (courtroom, church), informally (family, some classrooms), or would they be using an "in-group" language (party, street)? Would all the characters use the same style, or would some speak more formally than others?

Give the students a Scriptwriting worksheet (see p. 136) and have them use it to write a short script.

Improvisation with Tape Recorder

To begin this activity, have your students get in groups of three or four and improvise a scene from one of the prompts below or from prompts you create together as a class.

For younger students:

- getting blamed for something you didn't do
- experiencing the death of a pet
- being punished
- deciding whether or not to do something that might get you in trouble

For older students, any of the above, plus:

- breaking up with a boyfriend/girlfriend
- losing a job
- facing peer pressure on the street or at a party (drugs, alcohol, sex, guns)

Using either a tape recorder or a video camera, have one student record what the others improvise.

Play the tape back. Transcribe the dialogue, with each person writing down his or her own speech and the person who did the recording writing the actions.

Make a clean copy, and make a copy for everyone in the group.

Revise. Are all the speeches and the actions necessary? Would any additions make the script more interesting? Is everything in the right order?

Type up a final script and give everyone in the group a copy. Act out the script for the rest of the class.

Rewriting to Change the Script

We all do this: "If I had left home five minutes earlier, that might have been me in the traffic pileup I passed on the highway." Or, as we drive home from a meeting or a party: "I should have said . . ." This exercise gives a structure to that human impulse, allowing students to imagine a different outcome to an event or an ongoing situation.

You may find examples of such thinking in stories your students write. Michelle's story "How One Night Changed My Life Forever," (p. 84) explicitly states, "It all would've changed and been better if I just hadn't asked." Using such an example, ask your students to actively rewrite the script of a story or a scene.

Beginning with any piece of student writing (fiction, poetry, or nonfiction, as well as drama), look for places where things went wrong: a fight became inevitable, a friendship irreparable, a suicide difficult to prevent. Write a script of the same story, but show how it could take a different turn. For an example of how this might work, look at Shantell's script *Bob and Jan* (p. 113) and then at Scene 7 from *Why Darkness Seems So Light* (p. 116). Scene 7 is not a rewrite of any particular script, but it is based on a number of scripts written by high school or middle school girls, in which boys claimed more power than the girls wanted to give them. It is intentionally written in such a way as to put more control into the voice and the actions of the character Whitney.

One of the important things about writing is that students can slow things down and think about what they want to say and how they want to say it. Writing a dramatic script can help them gain control of a situation by thinking it through in slow motion. And rewriting a script can help them think about alternative endings: how one thing leads to another, in writing and in their lives.

Here is how a group of middle school students rewrote "I Remember Mrs. King" (p. 88):

IF MRS. KING WERE NICE
SETTING
Classroom, desks in rows, first day of school.

CHARACTERS

Mrs. King: *teacher, white*

Thomas: *fourth grader, 11, African American*

Juan: *fourth grader, 9½, mixed-race*

Kelley: *fourth grader, 9½, white*

LIGHTS UP

Kids come in, talking, laughing, looking for desks.

MRS. KING: *[Enters, looks around]* Would everyone please be quiet and take their seats?

KELLEY: You can't make me be quiet. You ain't my mama.

MRS. KING: Kelley, please be quiet. This is the first day of school. Let's not get off to a bad start.

KELLEY: O.K. *[Sits down]*

MRS. KING: Welcome to the first day of school. I'm very happy to have you here.

JUAN: I need a chair.

MRS. KING: Have a seat wherever you like.

JUAN: There's not enough desks.

MRS. KING: O.K. Juan, you will be my helper. Find out how many people still need chairs. *[Juan counts people and desks. Mrs. King writes a note and gives it to him.]* Take this to the office and get more desks.

JUAN: I don't know where to go. It's my first day.

THOMAS: Can I help him? I know where the office is.

MRS. KING: Sure.

When I heard these girls create this scene, I wanted every one of them to grow up to be a teacher. And I wanted every Mrs. King to see herself transformed in their imaginations.

Writing Dialogue in Different Styles of Speech

Try this yourself: listen carefully to your students' conversations and try to write down exactly what they say. Can you capture their youthful slang expressions, the lilt of their voices, the pace of their speech? If you have students who speak English as a second language or whose speech outside of class is not formal English, try writing a dialogue as you think they would speak it. It's harder than you might imagine!

When I was working on *Keesha's House* (see "White Walls" p. 69 and "I Look Around and Wonder" p. 71), I hired youth consultants to read the poems and help me get the language and the characters right. I have worked with teenagers for years and have listened carefully to their voices, but it was challenging for me to get it right in writing. In one of the consultations I said, "It's hard for me to make this sound right. I grew up talking kind of like they talk on the news, and I feel like a first grader in the language of some of my characters."

My young consultant said, "That's how school is for me most of the time." And then she generously helped me with every specific question about whether a character would say "they" or "their," "look" or "looks"; where the characters would drop their *g*s; and who would be likely to say "ain't" and in which situations. Every teacher should try to do this to learn firsthand how difficult it is to hear and write a speech pattern that doesn't "sound right" to you.

I would advise you to be cautious about asking your students to write in a style different from their own voice, because it's so hard to get it right. If it's not done with great respect and consideration, it can come out sounding stereotypical, which could be hurtful to other class members. But if students do try to write such dialogue, encourage them to recognize one another as resources. The English language, as spoken in different parts of America and the rest of the world, is beautifully varied. If you are lucky enough to have students who speak in a variety of styles, they can help one another create richly textured dialogue.

Jumping-Off Points

After your students have written individual or small-group scripts, suggest that they use those scenes to create new ones. A few ideas:

- Students form new groups and create a scene in which a character from one script meets a character from another.
- Students write a scene one year later in the lives of their own characters or one of their classmates' characters.
- Using characters from the writing examples you have shared with your class, students introduce them to each other to create a new script. Some possibilities from examples in this book:

  The speaker in "Watermelon Hill" meets Jan from "Bob and Jan."
  The speaker in "Pain" meets Rose from "Scene 5: Ginger and Rose."
  The friends in "Middle Sister Poem" meet each other five years later.
  The speaker in "I Remember Mrs. King" meets Mrs. King when he is a
      successful adult and she is an old woman.

The process of writing an entire play and performing it in front of an audience is an activity beyond the scope of this book, but if you want to try that I encourage you to do so, and I have listed resources in Appendix A to help you. Whether your students create a short script and read it in class to you and their fellow students or create and produce an entire stage or video production, the rewards of dramatic writing are immense.

Drama Examples: Student Writing

BOB AND JAN

Shantell wrote this script according to my suggestion that she write in parentheses anything Jan was thinking at the time. This isn't standard scriptwriting technique, but it can be useful in helping get a scene down on paper.

CHARACTERS
Bob *(16 years old)*
Jan *(14 years old)*
(Bob and Jan have been together for 6 or 7 months)
SETTING
Bedroom, late summer (August)
SCRIPT
BOB: I think it's a good idea. It will show me how much you love me.
JAN: Bob, you know I care for you a lot. I just don't think we're ready, or if I'm even ready for this. (I hope he doesn't start to get mad about this again.)
BOB: C'mon. Look, if you're afraid it will hurt, don't worry about it. I'll make sure you're not in any pain.
JAN: That's not what I'm worried about. I just am not sure if I want to.
BOB: *[Yelling, very mad]* Not want to! How could you not want to? I'm your boyfriend!
JAN: It's not you, Bob, it's . . .
BOB: *[Interrupting Jan, screaming]* It's the fact that you're just a little tease. I've waited almost 7 months for you and all we ever do is talk about it. It's so aggravating.
JAN: (oh no, here we go again) Bob, I can not believe you think that. I can't believe you'd even say that. I'm going home. Call me after you cool down if you want, or go find some other little tease!
BOB: No, you're not leaving. We're not done talking. *[Bob throws Jan on the bed and continues to yell.]* You don't know how much it hurts to be in my position. I deserve it after all I've been through.

JAN: (I really want to go home.) What you've been through! I can't believe this. *[Jan gets up and walks toward the door.]* Don't you think I feel bad? There is just so much stuff that can happen.

BOB: No, it won't.

JAN: Sometimes I wonder if you actually even care about me.

BOB: I can't . . . Ugh! You make me so mad!

JAN: Call me after you cool down.

BOB: No, we're not done talking. Why, why do you have to tease me like this?

JAN: I don't tease you, I . . .

BOB: *[Interrupting her again]* Oh, then what do you do?

JAN: I don't tease you.

BOB: *[Raises his hand and hits Jan]* Are we gonna or not?

JAN: *[Crying from the pain]* I guess.

As Bob forced himself on Jan, she began to cry even more. All she could hear was Bob's sister's music playing in the background. "Hero" by Mariah Carey.

Two weeks later they broke up, after another intense episode like this one.

—Shantell

Adult Writing

The following two scenes are from *Why Darkness Seems So Light* by Harvey Cocks and Helen Frost.

SCENE 5: GINGER AND ROSE

The character Ginger in this story is based, in part, on Michelle's story "How One Night Changed My Life Forever" (p. 84). In this scene, Ginger talks to her grandmother, Rose, the day after the party at which Ginger's friend was killed.

SETTING

Later that day. The pleasant kitchen/living room of ROSE's house. A table with three chairs is CENTER STAGE. To the RIGHT is an ironing board, to the LEFT a loveseat.

CHARACTERS

Ginger

Rose *(Ginger's Grandma)*

LIGHTS UP

ROSE is standing at an ironing board, ironing. There is a knock at the door, then the door opens before ROSE goes to answer.

GINGER: [*ENTERS*] Hi, Grandma. It's just me.

ROSE: Come on in, Sweetie. I just made some tea. Want some?

GINGER: No. [*Sits down at table.*]

ROSE: How's everything going?

GINGER: O.K.

ROSE: You sure? You seem worried.

GINGER: I'm okay. [*ROSE studies GINGER but doesn't ask any questions. Keeps ironing while GINGER sits in silence.*]

GINGER: Grandma, there's something I need to ask you.

ROSE: What's that?

GINGER: A friend of mine was wondering, and I thought you might know . . . Is there some way to get blood out of a shirt?

ROSE: [*Pauses, looks at GINGER a minute before answering, then goes back to her ironing as she answers.*] Well, yes. You use cold water. Hot water sets the stain, so don't wash it in hot water first. Sometimes you have to soak it awhile, or rub a little soap into it. [*She looks thoughtfully at GINGER for a minute, then continues.*] Is it a big stain or a little stain?

GINGER: Big.

ROSE: [*Carefully trying to get more information.*] What kind of material?

GINGER: Cotton.

ROSE: Ginger, you didn't get hurt, did you?

GINGER: [*Looks up quickly*] No, it's not my shirt. A friend of mine wants to know.

ROSE: What happened?

GINGER: Nothing. Don't worry about it.

ROSE: You know me better than that. I worry even when there's nothing to worry about, and this sounds like maybe I *should* be worried.

GINGER: [*Looks up at ROSE, considering.*] Well, don't tell Mom and Dad.

ROSE: Why don't you want them to know?

GINGER: I was somewhere I wasn't supposed to be. Dad would kill me.

ROSE: I doubt that.

GINGER: Well, you know what I mean.

ROSE: He's just trying to protect you.

GINGER: I know. But if I tell you what happened, don't tell him or Mom. Please?

ROSE: [*Puts down her iron, sits down at the table, pours a cup of tea.*] We'll see. What happened?

GINGER: I was with a boy who got shot last night. It's his blood on my shirt.

ROSE: Oh, my God. Is that the boy I read about in the paper?

GINGER: Yes.

ROSE: *[Sets down her tea. Takes a deep breath.]* Do you know who shot him?

GINGER: I don't know his name, but I think I could find out. I'll never forget his face. He looked really mean.

ROSE: *[After a pause.]* Maybe you *should* forget his face.

GINGER: What? Grandma, you always know exactly what's right and what's wrong. How can it be right not to tell the police what I saw? They're looking for witnesses.

ROSE: This is a dangerous person, Ginger. Don't get yourself involved in this.

GINGER: I'm already involved. I could call anonymously.

ROSE: It's too dangerous. Just stay out of it.

GINGER: He should be in jail. He might kill someone else.

ROSE: And that someone could be you!

GINGER: Grandma, Johnny had a gun, and I made him put it back in the car. *[Puts her head in her hands and starts to cry.]* It's my fault he was killed. He didn't even want to go to the party. I talked him into it.

ROSE: *[Gets up and stands behind Ginger, puts her arms around her.]* You had no way of knowing what would happen.

GINGER: It still happened.

ROSE: It's not your fault, honey. *[Moves over to the couch and fluffs up a pillow.]* Come on over here and rest for awhile.

GINGER: *[Goes over to the couch and curls up, clutching a stuffed bear.]* I just wish I could live yesterday all over again.

ROSE: [*Puts an afghan over GINGER, stands behind her, and puts her hand on GINGER's shoulder]* Oh, honey, we all wish that sometimes. *[Hums a quiet song. BLACKOUT.]*

End of Scene 5

This excerpt from the script may be reproduced for classroom use only. If you wish to purchase the play or obtain the rights to perform these scenes or the play in front of an audience, contact Pioneer Drama Service, Inc., P.O. Box 4267, Englewood, CO 80155-4267.

SCENE 7: MARCUS AND WHITNEY

In the scene before this one, Whitney tells her sister that she is going to Laser-Zone with Marcus but that she just wants to be friends with him.

CHARACTERS

Whitney: *teenage girl*

Marcus: *teenage boy*

Nathan: *Marcus' younger brother*
SETTING
Evening. In front of Laser-Zone.
LIGHTS UP
There is LOUD MUSIC and FLASHING LIGHTS. SOUNDS of LASER-TAG come from OFFSTAGE. The MUSIC becomes quieter as WHITNEY and MARCUS ENTER. NATHAN trails behind a few paces.

NATHAN: Are you about ready to go Marcus? We've been here for two hours.
MARCUS: Leave us alone for awhile, Nate. I'll let you know when it's time to leave.
NATHAN: O.K. I'll be over there with Art. *[He EXITS.]*
WHITNEY: I'm ready to leave now. This was a lot of fun, but I'm supposed to be home in 15 minutes.
MARCUS: A few minutes won't matter. Here, I got you a Coke. *[Offers can.]* Come over and sit down for awhile.
WHITNEY: Here is fine. *[Indicates near the lights and side of the stage that the noise is coming from.]*
MARCUS: No, I want to get away from all the noise. Come over here. *[WHITNEY accepts the Coke, but sits down where she wants to, near Laser-Zone. MARCUS picks up her Coke and moves to another table, farther away. She follows him and sits down across the table from him.]* Sit over here. I won't bite.
WHITNEY: I'm fine here. *[MARCUS moves to where she is sitting and puts his arm around her. WHITNEY gets up and moves away from him.]* I don't want to start that again, Marcus.
MARCUS: Sure you do.
WHITNEY: No, I told you. I just want to be friends.
MARCUS: Can't a friend get a little hug now and then?
WHITNEY: Well, I guess, just a little hug. *[She hugs MARCUS and he pulls her to the chair and sits down, pulling her onto his lap.]*
MARCUS: I've really missed you, Whitney. I can't stop thinking about you. *[Tries to kiss her.]*
WHITNEY: Stop it, Marcus. I don't want to do this. *[Gets up and moves away.]*
MARCUS: You always say that. I know you don't mean it.
WHITNEY: I do mean it. This was why I broke up with you! Things were moving too fast. You promised it would be different tonight.
MARCUS: It *will* be different. Let me show you. You'll like this. *[He kisses her as she tries to turn her head away.]*
WHITNEY: Stop it. You're hurting me.

MARCUS: You know I wouldn't hurt you. I love you.

WHITNEY: Let me go! *[He keeps kissing her, and holds her so her arms are pinned. She breaks free.]*

MARCUS: I just can't help myself. You look so fine in that outfit.

WHITNEY: Can't I look nice without you attacking me?

MARCUS: *[Beginning to get angry.]* Hey, now, I'm not attacking you. This is just the way guys are.

WHITNEY: Well, I'm leaving.

MARCUS: Just one more kiss.

WHITNEY: No!

MARCUS: I'm going to get what I can from you before we break up for good. *[He pushes WHITNEY roughly onto the table, pins her down, and starts kissing her again. She kicks at the table, trying to attract attention.]*

WHITNEY: Help me! Someone help me!

NATHAN: *[ENTERS, runs over and jumps on MARCUS' back and pulls him off WHITNEY.]* What are you doing, man? Leave the girl alone!

MARCUS: Hey, we're not doing anything. Just having a little fun.

NATHAN: Doesn't sound like she's having fun.

MARCUS: Mind your own business. *[Pushes NATHAN aside.]* Just leave us alone.

NATHAN: I'll leave you alone if you leave her alone.

MARCUS: You've already ruined everything. Just get out of here. *[NATHAN exits, looking back over his shoulder at MARCUS and WHITNEY.]* Let's go. Come on, I'll take you home.

WHITNEY: I'm not going home with you. I'm calling my dad.

MARCUS: O.K. Fine. *[Shrugs]* I'm outta here. *[He EXITS, angry. WHITNEY crosses her arms, looks up, shudders, then slumps, in a gesture of relief. BLACKOUT]*

End of Scene 7

Appendix A

RESOURCES FOR TEACHING WRITING

Hundreds of books, websites, and organizations offer support to teachers of writing; this list of resources is by no means comprehensive. It is rather a gathering of a few personal favorites that I hope will be helpful to you.

Good Starting Points

Teachers & Writers Collaborative publishes a bimonthly newsletter and offers workshops and support for teachers and writers in schools. The T&W catalog and website offer a wide selection of resources about teaching writing.

5 Union Square West
New York, NY 10003-3306
(212) 691-6590 or toll-free (888) BOOKS-TW
http://www.twc.org/

Heinemann offers support for teachers of writing through books, teacher workshops, and web-based courses.

361 Hanover Street
Portsmouth, NH 03801-3912
1-800-541-2086
Books and workshops: www.heinemann.com
Web-based courses: www.HeinemannU.com

Books and a Website About Teaching Writing (no specific genre)

Kohl, Herbert. 1994. *I Won't Learn From You and Other Thoughts on Creative Maladjustment*. New York. The New Press.

Marzán, Julio, editor. 1996. *Luna, Luna: Creative Writing Ideas from Spanish, Latin American, and Latino Literature*. New York: Teachers & Writers Collaborative.

Thomas, Lorenzo. 1998. *Sing the Sun Up: Creative Writing Ideas from African American Literature*. New York: Teachers & Writers Collaborative.

Voices From the Gaps, an instructional website focusing on the lives and works of North American women writers of color. <http://voices.cla.umn.edu/>

Books and Websites About Poetry

Harper, Michael S. and Anthony Walton, editors. 1994. *Every Shut Eye Ain't Asleep: An Anthology of Poetry by African Americans Since 1945*. New York: Little, Brown and Company.

Heard, Georgia. 1999. *Awakening the Heart: Exploring Poetry in Elementary and Middle School*. Portsmouth, NH: Heinemann.

Moyers, Bill, editor. 1995. *The Language of Life*. New York: Doubleday. (Poems and interviews with poets, a number of whom discuss and write about abuse, racial discrimination, depression, prison, and other difficult issues). Also a PBS series, available as a series of videos.

Nye, Naomi Shihab, editor. 2000. *Salting the Ocean: 100 Poems by Young Poets*. New York: HarperCollins (Greenwillow).

Contemporary American Poetry Archive, a website where out of print books by contemporary American poets are available in their entirety. <http://capa.concoll.edu>

Electronic Poetry Center@SUNY Buffalo, a good starting point for information about poetry, and links to other poetry sites. <http://epc.buffalo.edu/>

Books About Nonfiction

Frost, Helen, editor. 1999. *Why Darkness Seems So Light: Young People Speak Out About Violence*. Pecan Grove Press.

Gruwell, Erin and The Freedom Writers. 1999. *The Freedom Writers Diary*. New York: Doubleday (Main Street Books).

Pollack, William S. 2000. *Real Boys' Voices*. New York: Penguin Books.

Books About Fiction

Bauer, Marion Dane. 1992. *What's Your Story*. New York: Houghton Mifflin.

———. 1996. *Our Stories: A Fiction Workshop for Young Authors*. New York: Houghton Mifflin. (Companion volume to *What's Your Story*.)

Schaefer, Lola M. 2000. *Teaching Narrative Writing: The Tools That Work for Every Student: Grades 4–8*. New York: Scholastic.

Books About Drama

Kohl, Herbert. 1995. *Making Theater: Developing Plays with Young People*. New York: Teachers & Writers Collaborative.

Sklar, Daniel Judah. 1995. *Playmaking: Children Writing and Performing Their Own Plays*. New York: Teachers & Writers Collaborative.

Resource for Publishing Student Writing

There are numerous printing companies that will print self-published books, and some that offer various levels of support for self-publishers. One that I have used is Morris Publishing (minimum of two hundred copies). It has options for cover designs and can include photographs and illustrations. Write or call well in advance for details.

Morris Publishing
3212 East Highway 30
Kearney NE 68847
1-800-650-7888
www.morrispublishing.com

Appendix B

LITERATURE THAT ADDRESSES PROBLEMS

Here are a few books that may help young people through troubling times, and/or help you understand what your students are going through. Keep your own list of favorites and encourage your students to do the same. (The parenthetical subjects are over-simplifications.)

For Children

Greer, Colin and Herbert Kohl. 1995. *A Call to Character*. New York: HarperCollins. (a good source of selections for reading aloud)

MacLachlan, Patricia. 1987. *Sarah, Plain and Tall*. New York: HarperCollins. (stepparent)

———. 1995. *Baby*. New York: Dell Yearling. (death of a sibling, power of poetry)

———. 1993. *Journey*. New York: Dell Yearling. (desertion by a parent)

Mikaelsen, Ben. *Petey*. New York: Hyperion. (cerebral palsy, unrecognized intelligence)

Myers, Walter Dean. 1988. *Scorpions*. New York: HarperCollins. (lure of gangs)

———. 1983. *Hoops*. New York: Delacorte. (basketball, hard choices)

Paterson, Katherine. 1994. *The Flip-Flop Girl*. New York: HarperCollins. (death of a parent, voiceless anger)

———. 1997. *Bridge to Terabithia*. New York: HarperCollins. (death of a friend)

———. 1987. *The Great Gilly Hopkins*. New York: HarperCollins. (foster care, fantasy of finding real mother)

Ryan, Pam Munoz. 1997. *Riding Freedom*. New York: Scholastic. (raised as orphan, finding courage)

Sachar, Louis. 1998. *Holes*. Farrar, Straus & Giroux. (juvenile detention)

Spinelli, Jerry. 1992. *Maniac McGee*. New York: HarperCollins. (race, street life, runaways)

Taylor, Mildred D. 1976. *Roll of Thunder, Hear My Cry*. New York: Dial.

———. 1981. *May the Circle be Unbroken*. New York: Dial.

———. 1990. *The Road To Memphis*. New York: Dial. (racism, violence, loyalty to family and friends)

For your own reading, or to share with very mature students: Books dealing with incest and child abuse.

Banks, Russell. 1996. *Rule of the Bone*. New York: HarperCollins.

Sapphire. 1996. *Push*. New York: Vintage.

Silverman, Sue William. 1999. *Because I Remember Terror, Father, I Remember You*. Athens, Georgia: University of Georgia Press.

Appendix C

EXAMPLES IN THIS BOOK, LISTED ACCORDING TO TOPIC

Violence

"Kerosene," by Tim Seibles (p. 66)

"How One Night Changed My Life Forever," by Michelle (p. 84)

"'The Universe Is a Safe Place for Souls'," by Jeff Gundy (p. 90)

"Day of Sadness," by Mindy (p. 64)

"Pain," by Tony (p. 84)

"Bob and Jan," by Shantell (p. 113)

"Scene 5: Ginger and Rose," by Harvey Cocks and Helen Frost (p. 114)

"Scene 7: Marcus and Whitney," by Harvey Cocks and Helen Frost (p. 116)

Sexuality

"Watermelon Hill," by Linda Back McKay (p. 68)

"I Look Around and Wonder," by Helen Frost (p. 71)

"Natonya's Night Wishes," by Erskina (p. 101)

"Bob and Jan," by Shantell (p. 113)

"Scene 7: Marcus and Whitney," by Harvey Cocks and Helen Frost (p. 116)

Juvenile Detention

Suicide

Family

Friends

Race

Alcohol

"White Walls," by Helen Frost (p. 69)

School

"I Remember Mrs. King," by Ketu Oladuwa (p. 88)

"'The Universe Is a Safe Place for Souls'," by Jeff Gundy (p. 90)

Comfort

"Sap," by Beth Simon (p. 91)

"Almost Dead," by Alyssa (103)

"Eat Dirt," by Constance García-Barrio (p. 106)

Appendix D
WORKSHEETS

IMAGE WORKSHEET

Images
Write details to make an image.

who, what   does this
_____   _____

Details   **Details**
how big?   how?

what color(s)?   where?

what kind?   when (season, time of day)?

what else?   what else?

Choose from those details to create an image in the space below.

CONVERSATION WITH A FEELING WORKSHEET

Talking to my _____ (name a feeling)

When (write something that happened)

My _____(feeling, same as in title) *was like*

I spoke to my _____(feeling) *and said*

And it answered

I answered back

TRITINA WORKSHEET

Tritina Form

_____ Word A

_____ Word B

_____ Word C

_____ Word C

_____ Word A

_____ Word B

_____ Word B

_____ Word C

_____ Word A

_____ Use all three words.

DETAILS OF THE SENSES WORKSHEET

Sight   Sound

Taste   Smell

Touch   "Sixth Sense"

WRITING ABOUT VIOLENCE
PREWRITING WORKSHEET

Describe the event in one or two sentences:

Where did this event take place?

What was the weather like? Give specific details that will show this: a snow shovel, a sweaty T-shirt, an umbrella.

Was it indoors or outdoors? Give details that will show this: furniture, trees, traffic, windows, animals (pets or wild animals).

Do you remember any colors?

Sounds?

Smells?

Tastes or textures?

What people were there? How were they related to each other?

Was there a conflict?

Do you remember any dialogue or anything someone said?

Did anyone have power over anyone else?

WRITING ABOUT VIOLENCE
PREWRITING WORKSHEET (continued)

Was anyone bigger or stronger?

Was territory part of the problem?

How about race?

Gender?

Love?

Was there a particular point when the situation turned from conflict to violence?

Was someone hurt? How seriously?

What were/are the long-term effects?

Could you have done anything to change the outcome?

Could someone else have done anything to change the outcome?

Write anything else you want to write about this. If you learned something from it, write a little bit about that.

RIVER OF CHOICES WORKSHEET

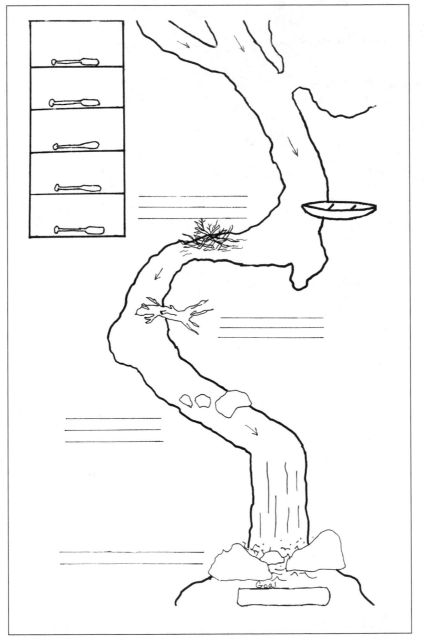

FICTION WRITING WORKSHEET

Jot down a few notes in response to these questions:

1. Who is your main character? What do your readers need to know about this person in order to understand what happens in the story? What is important to the character? (Some of the things listed here may not matter in your story — you decide.)
   name:
   age:
   male or female:
   appearance:
   family:
   rich or poor:
   anything else:

2. Where does the story happen? Use details to describe a specific place. You can use details from a place (or places) you know to create a place in your imagination.

   Does most of the story take place indoors or outdoors?
   What is the weather like?

3. How does the story begin? What happens?

4. How does your character feel about what happens? What does the character do or say to show these feelings?

On another page, write a story. Use your notes to guide you, but let your imagination go wherever it takes you.

SCRIPTWRITING WORKSHEET

Title _____

Author (your name) _____

Setting (description of the place where the scene happens):

Characters (names and brief descriptions):

"Lights up" or "Opening shot" (what is happening at the beginning of the scene):

Dialogue (As each character speaks, give the character's name, followed by a colon. Write exactly what they say. If they do something, write the action in parentheses.):

Continue on for as many pages as you need. At the end, write "End of Scene."